The Glamour Poet Versus……

Selected Publications by Jeremy Reed

Poetry

Isthmus of Samuel Greenberg (1976)
Bleecker Street (1980)
By The Fisheries (1984)
Nero (1985)
Selected Poems (1987)
Engaging Form (1988)
Nineties (1990)
Red Haired Android (1992)
Kicks (1994)
Pop Stars, with Mick Rock (1995)
Sweet Sister Lyric (1996)
Saint Billie (2000)
Patron Saint of Eyeliner (2000)
Heartbreak Hotel (2002)
Duck and Sally Inside (2006)
Orange Sunshine (2006)
This Is How You Disappear (2007)
West End Survival Kit (2009)
Bona Drag (2009)
Black Russian: Out-takes from the Airmen's Club 1978-9 (2010)
Piccadilly Bongo (with Marc Almond) (2010)
Bona Vada (2011)
Whitehall Jackals (with Chris McCabe) (2013)

Novels

The Lipstick Boys (1984)
Blue Rock (1987)
Red Eclipse (1989)
Inhabiting Shadows (1990)
Isidore (1991)
When The Whip Comes Down (1992)
Chasing Black Rainbows (1994)
The Pleasure Chateau (1994)
Diamond Nebula (1995)
Red Hot Lipstick (1996)
Sister Midnight (1997)
Dorian (1998)
Boy Caesar (2004)
The Grid (2008)
Here Comes the Nice (2011)

The Glamour Poet Versus Francis Bacon, Rent and Eyelinered Pussycat Dolls

Jeremy Reed

Shearsman Books

Published in the United Kingdom in 2014 by
Shearsman Books Ltd

www.shearsman.com

ISBN 978-1-84861-323-2
First Edition

for John Robinson and Mark Jackson with love

Waiting for the Man

80mm

My palm's mapped like the London underground,
a network into which I crushed the blues,
an 80mm clenched left hand

pocketed, dusty with Diazepam
I'd lick off, panicked when the tube went dead
between two stops, 50 metres below

street level on jumpy Northern Line track
630 VDC traction voltage
the line colour coded corporate black.

Submerged in panic I'd fry in neurons,
cold sweat collecting like white grapes, my tongue
furred by the blue food colouring extract (FDXC Blue No2)

coating the granules licked to residue
feeding a habit I was pulled inside
like a pressurized cabin door. I'd cook

down there, reading the dot-matrix display,
pilled-up accelerated by the rush
under the city and projecting hard

into a stranger's eyes to hold and keep
their fascination—a skinny poet
with pop star looks selling sex and a mix

of spiked-up glittered personality
and hot neural poetry—I could write
a poem directly in someone's face

like sci-fi owning to reality,
the imagery metabolised like pills,
the fast impacted energies a cosh

to mainstream greys—I switched to the blue line,
got off at Piccadilly, back to air
and busy abstract figures of sunshine.

The man's eyes at the top of the steps were grey.
I didn't know how many eyes he'd looked
into that way
today or any other. They turned blue
close up. 'The Regent Palace' what he said,
'I'll pay you twice over you know
to blow
your looks, I get so lonely see so low
below
the city, it's not sex it's you honey
I
need to fill that space money can't buy,
I try not to keep hanging round this place
I'll look
after you if you need, a hundred right?
Don't go
I need
you so, the money's for a start
I'm Joe

Diazepam
Systematic (IUPAC) name
7—chloro —1—methyl—
5—phenyl—1, 3—dihydro—2H—
1—4 benzodiazepin—2—one

data shaped like the metaphysically articulated construct
of a stanza pattern tooled by John
Donne—
length-to-width ratio
like a blue diamond's angles
the white light inside
like earth seen from the moon
'Do you?'
he said [Joe]
'give head, blow?'

The room at the Regent Palace Hotel—white clinical
walls, refrigerator white, alienating as the International
Space Station, the insulated hotel noise like brain-chatter
when you're aware of resistance to sleep. The room was
on the 9th floor, the windows nailed down, black duct
tape on the floor holding the edges of a no-colour carpet
flat. 91 bedrooms and each of them a foreign
space, like Trojan asteroids densely clustering in
Jupiter's orbit or a mapping of grey matter across
the brain. It was how I imagined death to be if
there was a post-biological precinct for individual
consciousness, with Sherwood Street outside facing
down the full-on grainy West End day.

Rent Boy Blues

Your metzas smell
of Dilly loot
there's semen polished
on your boot
the things you do
to me aren't cute
and leave me blue

I'm bona vada
bona drag
bona riah
with a handbag
the things you do
to me aren't cute
and leave me blue

I'm spotty mean
and dressed in black
a runaway teen
on the meat rack
the things you do
to me aren't cute
and leave me blue

I buy a pizza
feed my habit
burn a hole
inside my pocket
the things you do
to me aren't cute
and leave me blue

I'm outside Boots
I speak polari
but to your taste
I'm just salami

The things you do
to me aren't cute
and leave me blue

You want me daddy
I'm rough trade
broken damaged
and afraid
the things you do
to me aren't cute
and leave me blue

I've got no option
and maybe three years
a Dilly boy
age in arrears
The things you do
to me aren't cute
and leave me blue

I can't go home
they tell me Johnny
you're drugs and rent
and messed up honey
The things you do
to me aren't cute
and leave me blue

Bowie Looks

The similarities in looks
helium-lifted cheek bones pointing
right to the eyes, the alien gene
provoking ambiguity
the Thin White Duke instructing a Gitanes
and me strung out at Piccadilly

the analogies always there
Bowie circa 1976
both of us projecting close encounter
contact, a lateral shift
wide of human, up on sex,
two-tone eyes and two tone hair

re-modified human appeal
tripping up gay and straight.
Bowie's Weimar aesthetic burnt
a bullet hole through style, white shirt,
black waistcoat, size zero, a hat
so Gatsby angled that it hurt

by oversubscribed panache.
I was the head-turner who pulled
one out of three into my face
as tricky big-city curious
looking like I'd dropped in from space
with attitude—my stage the street—

a Bowie soundtrack in my head
for aural company
when making tracks on poetry
there in the crowd, I wrote for speed
of strangers moving through my words
like shooting a movie

before writing the bits down
in a café on Glasshouse Street

to mix the imagery hot,
immediate, 'Sound and Vision'
fading in and out my mind
as a blue-themed backup to what I'd got.

Chemical Data

Formula C - - H, CIN, O
Mol. mass 284.7 g/mol
Pharmacokinetic data
Bioavailability 93%
Metabolism Hepatic
Half life 20-100 hours

Cocksucker Blues

'You're smack' Joe said
115 lbs
conversion by the drug,
his body's angular pretzel
territorializing the bed

his one concession to colour
hexagonal patterned Burlington socks
in diamond charcoal pink and red
extraneous as puppets,
his crumpled Saks 5th Avenue suit bled

over a chair, satin lining
the colour of an oyster shell.
'Use H baby and you'll be dead'
Joe gestured to the wall,
first-pass effect if it's oral,

injected it goes rapid-fire
through the blood-brain barrier
launch-padding histamine.
His desperation attracted
my sense of being family

to every outsider whose edge
gravitated to my looks
corner of Shaftesbury Avenue
the sky aerospace silver—
I told him the real me wrote books

the sort nobody ever reads:
poetry, and I'd use him too
as protein to my imagery.
Loneliness sucked him into a black hole,
his Hardy Amies tie a blue

I'd only seen in hydrangeas,
Joe paying for my company
to be himself and every week
Wednesday 3pm at the hotel
his confessional intimacy

comes up as an acute need,
his presents jumpers, shirts, cologne
filling in a space for me
both of us nurturing dependencies,
damaged, afraid, frightened to be alone.

Eye-Count

I gave up my eye-count—300 contacts a day as
hits. I couldn't save them in memory, and wondered if
I was still on replay in someone's virtual recall, a boy or
girls I'd got into through the eyes that were variants of
blue, green, grey, brown, hazel. Was somebody still
doing neural photoshops on manipulating my image, hours,
days after we'd met, like a hologram?
And you
the face I always wanted slipped away
dissolved into anonymity
'Blue blue electric blue
that's the colour of the room
where I will live'

'You're gay'
the punter said, 'that thin
it's hero
in
it's such a give away
you stick a spike into a vein.' The rain
opened up like China, I saw him washed
into the underground, white Burberry saturated grey.

‘The encounters between queer urban culture and the law ensured that public knowledge of homosexuality was framed by an overarching narrative of sexual danger. If that danger was located in different qualities and influences, these were all, nonetheless, underpinned by a common assumption: the queer threatened British society.’

Matt Houlbrook, *Queer London*

Microgeography

The Dilly as a microgeography. An addict to its groove
I knew complemented his obsession with the place by
circulating a hand-drawn map of rent locale from
the north side of Piccadilly circus, under the arches,
extending to Leicester Square, a ventricular imaging
of its underground resources. The conversion of [John's]
physical body into place, like buying real estate on
the moon, was the attempt to broker power over
fetishised geography. He's say to me that when he died
he'd need to shift the virtual equivalent of the place
with him, almost as a death-kit instruction manual,
as his identity was so compactly built into the place. You
can cross a continent exploring the subway exits and
each time encounter a different reality: Regent Street
isn't Shaftesbury Avenue or Glasshouse Street the Haymarket,
then north side might be tilted into shadow the south
confected with hazy arcs of turquoise and lipstick pink
sky fuzzed by CO^2 emissions over the Haymarket and
St James', while north-east over the Shaftesbury Memorial
Fountain there's an anthology of nitrogen dioxide (No2)
particles, carbon monoxide from vehicular exhaust and
West along Piccadilly a sky smudged by hydrocarbon fuel
vapours but pistachio-blue slung over with clouds like
the marks left by a cat's paws on the white enamel top of
a washing machine. The map measured 4x4 and
was printed dark blue on white with red dots indicating
places for rent and the existence of a constantly reinvented
gay subculture. I saw the place through poetry and
pills, a neurochemical interaction that ramped-up my
perceptions of the precinct into private mythology. Nobody
hangs out there long right in the city's heartbeat—you're
an outlaw, an urban folklore drop out, a missing person
in missing time, a fact gone offline with no credible ID.

North Side Lament

The sunlight turns gold on my skin—
I live on wine and Valium
it leaves me thin
I never knew I'd do
the things I do to you
as anyone, I'm blue

I sell to write my books
I tell them that, my looks
are wasted, if you're sensitive
you see through me
my neural network maps
amazing poetry

I never have contempt
for clients, they're events
who pay for company
I fine-tune a line
it sometimes makes me feel
real as orange sunshine

north side of the Circus
targeting my brain.
I never lose my cool
I write above it all
I'm dissociated
eyes blue as a swimming pool

saturated with imagery
like pop video
I'm waiting for the change
you'll re-arrange in me
of course the things I do
are always poetry

they make the speed of light
into reality

dreaming with my eyes open
by the subway steps
you'll pick me up as token
of my poetry

Piccadilly Delta

The first day I visited the Dilly the place came to
meet me—my expectations met by a man
immediately sighting me from the bottom of an entrance
staircase, a red, white and blue London Underground
roundel fixture above the stairs. The charge in the
air was like holding a gun, the big-city gravitational
pull reaching into my abdomen, as though the excitement
centred there in an electromagnetic field. It was the
drenched atmospherics of the place saturated me, the
unstoppable momentum of accelerated bodies all pointed
somewhere I didn't know—their eyes breaking up on
contact.

'You work here?' the man
        said
'I can take you back to mine
and make you a pop star—you've got the looks

it takes—go down on me—
        you'll see

Pistachio John Smedley cardigan—4.30 p.m. blue sky-coloured
skinny jeans, a gold chain demonstratively escaped the
crew neck of a clinically white T shirt, the catchlights in
his grey eyes churning money—I stonewalled the man—so
that my absence of response sounded like he was miked
in the studio. I watched him go make a reconnaissance
of the Circus, his loneliness the colour of fog on a harbour.
He kept turning round and looking over at me like I'd change
my mind and go find him. And out of curiosity I
was compelled to keep on finding him in the crowd like
some sort of visual hoodoo. The light was powdery gold
dusted with pollutants. There were boys hanging out on the
railings in the sunlight, but the man only had eyes for
me. He kept on sighting me and I him as a compulsive

reflex, a hex,
I shouldn't have been there
doing sexual voodoo
reinventing myself for poetry
taking the word into the underground
like the light in a ruby's interior
or a blue
morning glory opening on the breath—

I never got it right—some books in my bag—
Robert Duncan, Jack Spicer, Tom Clark—always trying
to learn ways of worrying the word into new
starbursts of imagery believing poetry could chart
like a pop song
and lyricise the West End
alley by alley into altered state shine. The man came
back on me, his gold chain fidgety like lightning, the
chunky swank of metal incongruous with his thin
aesthetic. I went back downstairs below the street
and stood on the underground concourse to wait for someone
out of the crowd I didn't know
to find me as my poetry, the two an inseparable
identity.
Girls came on at me, the ones with black thunder storms
of mascara, tailed eyeliner, researched faces
dusted with shimmer, the ones looking for vulnerability in
a man as the gateway
in
I took a 10mg blues to get the station right with a Valium
blue tint. Poetry doesn't help the blues, it's like track
marks left on the skin as epidermal hieroglyphics—a
language of disconnect I write
in
Heroin
opening a white tide in my blood on other afternoons,

thin
as a poppy stem and down again
diazepam
transmitting a blue flash, a colour I went in search
of, a poppy blue, contrail blue, vodka blue, the blue
lining to thought attached to poetry, a Viagra
blue, a consensus of blues that come up as the
colour of imagination
blue
like a poet's eyes are blue from colouring up imagery.

Looking, you go inside what you can never keep.
Whatever I sold I never gave away. Whoever came
at me had to cross 200 foggy sea miles reaching from
my birthplace to Piccadilly Circus. A blue-green arc
that hung on me as an aura.

The hurt in me goes deep
as the blues raw roots
a pain
like sugarcane mantras
at the Piccadilly Delta.
I can show you that my heart's
like a cracked ruby
my shot down amygdala
like a decommissioned plane.
I wait out the sparkling rain
for you Joe, Jim,
Johnny, it's you again
Billy like orbital mechanics
of the star-littered galaxy
lonely as Alpha Centauri
gravitating to the Circus
as an indifferent space
nobody there for him
just personalised public space

the way up the way down
to the limbic underground
a compulsive fall
criminal, abject, hypnotic,
as though the escalator down
terminated in a giant
scintillating Bakerloo line
shocking pink glitter ball

I got the pharmaceutical blue flash colour I
needed: Indigotine, allura red AC—a blue
that goes beyond Viagra blue into the neurochemical
uniqueness of my imagery.
Follow the leader

1) 'You Have' a rain-diced Marc Almond torch song based in the Soho alleys off the then Raymond Revuebar at 11 Walker's Court, a song for a dead boy, the vocal lifting the rain-drenched gutter into the sky.

2) 'Piccadilly Palare' as the one-time Morrissey let his knowledge of the railings out, the black paint flaking off his tongue, the song punching the criminal into pop.

3) 'What Have I Done To Deserve This?' The compassionate colour (pink or blue) in Dusty Springfield's tone injects a gay subtext into what could be an indigenous rent theme.

4) 'Cocksucker Blues' a raw bluesy Rolling Stones 1969 demo, Leicester Square based explicitly alienating rent-boy narrative, so lippily explicit it's stayed down.

5) 'Piccadilly Bongo' Expensive spoken word by Jeremy Reed with a menacing shuffling soundtrack from Itchy Ear and the rapaciously cruisy leather-coated Francis Bacon waiting by the subway gate.

6) 'Girl Don't Come' — a waiting song pivotal to melodic pop as loss — all rent boys feel stood up permanently in their waiting and Sandie Shaw's saturated black mascara and China black fringe gave a look to being stood up.

7) 'London Boys' a David Bowie pills and acceptance into the gang, a coterie of Mods on Wardour Street that connects with the Dilly network through Brewer Street—spotty seventeen in the song and nineteen outside, recorded in a demo session at R.G. Jones studios on October 18, 1966.

8) 'Dilly Boys' — was Pete Doherty with his dandified style and red nail varnish ever rent? The speculation's in the look and in a song in which he's 'the sweetest girl in the world,' communicate signals.

Dilly Top Ten

Marc Almond	You Have
Morrissey	Piccadilly Palare
Dusty Springfield	What Have I Done To Deserve This?
The Rolling Stones	Cocksucker Blues
The Ginger Light	Piccadilly Bongo
Sandie Shaw	Girl Don't Come
David Bowie	London Boys
The Libertines	Dilly Boys
The Only Ones	Out There In The Night
The Pretty Things	Honey I Need

Love for Sale

If you live outside convention, as I do, and you've worked as rent,
          as I have
you've an uncopyable subject matter for poetry. I'm
risking bringing the criminalised underworld in my life into poetry,
          a rogue gene.
Just as each time you breathe you bring the world
into and out yourself, so every time I've sold myself
to write and eat (note the order) I've attracted someone
in on the in breath and turned them out on the out
breath. It's an urban rhythm, the unrepeatable exchange
of transient contact in big-city life. The Arts do nothing
for poets, and I turned out of the
necessity to write to a support system that helped maintain
me through the illicit co-dependency of outlawed London needs.
All I wanted was the time to do what I do best
write poetry. You can't convincingly write about my
world unless you've been there
                    bright and in despair
vulnerable as somebody dreaming with their eyes open in
the unstoppable acceleration of crowds. I learnt to create
my own island on the pavement and to be sovereign to
that disputed constantly disrupted precinct. I was king to a radius
          on which
I dreamt and had to earn, when it rained the patch
darkened, it was rubbed out by the tide. What I did
was disinformation except to the ones in on it and
they never learnt my name, only remembered the colour
of my eyes as like a summer afternoon in the south,
two turquoise pigmented irises processing that weird
stuff poetry, like the galaxy's self-regulating system
of a hundred billion stars, as an industry for making
hot blue stars—or rather, a deep space
ecology. The Dilly was also symbolically off-earth: if you
went there for why I was there re-entry was never back
into any systemized reality.

Glamorous Glue

The skinny T-shirt's breathed on fit
matte black a faded black
charcoal under the arms
the sit
a Piccadilly look, a style

by accident and all I'd got
dripping with poetry
as unconvertible currency,
a black T-shirt so tight it hurt
my ribs like two black slatted islands

bumped out from my skin.
Just one punter I'd tell myself
and I could write next day
the sale hard as a diamond
cutting in me like grit—

the man pleading 'please stay',
you're all I've got,
loneliness churning in his eyes
like piled up cumulus
a sticky helix of glamorous glue

tracked on his shirt
as an opalescent signature
he'd come before the hurt
of solo life kicked in again
as a nagging alert

to visceral pain.
I'd go back to my cooky flat
his details in my pocket
and stand there in the aqua light
telling myself a poet

as an outlaw had to eat
to subvert a city
indifferent to that need,
the soles on my black All Star Converse
worn into my feet.

A Matter of Trust

It's a matter of trust a face in the crowd. I learnt to
beam in on the glitter of catchlights in the pupils
where the concentration of personality shows. Trust is
usually established by meeting in a stranger's eyes a light
one imagines in one's own. The dodgy go for a reciprocal
lights out, a mutual opacity. It's an instinctual micro-
second immediacy. A matter of life and death. I call
it eye stabbing—
                                        blue on brown or green on grey
                                        a reflex palette mixed
                                        intrinsically at speed of light
my way. You're in my life so suddenly I never knew
you or the things you do
                                                as you
and me, I've come so far on a journey to be the me
you'll never know, the things I write turn over in a
chemistry
                                          called poetry.
I could hate you but I need money to hide my hurt-in
poetry. There's nothing lower on the social list than
                                          poetry—
its place kept down with what the river never shows
as undertow. I read it though like no-one else, fists
full of scarlet sequins at a microphone, emoting, so
dynamic that you'd think it pop: you're not the first
or last today,
                                        if your name's really Ray
then open up your loneliness, it's there I'll meet you
in that damaged space: we've come together because
we don't fit anywhere in this city but under the
stairs at Piccadilly

                                          right down there

you think I'm class, I've got aesthetic and I write
a hurt into availability, I'm broken where you
are, it's easy—I'm class see—he's rent Johnny

with the blond hair over there outside Boots, a tough
provincial wannabe—there's a song about generic Johnnies—
Marc Almond's 'Stories Of Johnny'—a smoky jewel
picked out in lyric
                                        I don't feel a trust
to take you anywhere, see you another time maybe outside
or in my poetry: my mood has turned to rain.

White Bear and Francis Bacon

You got in from the Piccadilly exit stairs, a subterranean
bar in the underground, compact lowlight, red shaded
lamps, impersonal ambience, the updraft of the tube's
accelerated whine as feedback into the place like
shock waves from urban catastrophe. I used to hang out
in there writing myself into poetry, my laser-
directed focused concentration distressing the solitary
men in the room as unbreakable. It was there that I'd
meet him, every two or three weeks by arrangement, as
a distraction to our work—
                                        Francis Bacon
who'd entered my life through reading my student
novel The Lipstick Boys, an imploded, hallucinated
account of confused shook up youth on white beaches
                        under thundery pine-green
                        skies, his eyes blued into mine
                        foggier pigment in their mix,
                        their shine glittered with neuro-
                          endocrine chemistry
(what tone did we give each other's eyes imaginatively!)
                      and always the envelope of money
                      for me to write   £800 cash
                                  'sweetheart
                                  to help you write, poets
                                  need luxuries not necessities'—
he brought his own bottles in a carrier Dom Perignon,
Cristal, Château Pétrus, the barman never looked
we didn't care, down there under the street, he told
me every ventricle in his heart was blocked, asthma
locked into his chest, his bronchia like the unventilated
underground, the wheeze inflected with camp. When
you write to retrieve bits it's sometimes because you missed
their significance first time round and later they come
back as how it really was and happened. Bacon's cratered
face was a map of Soho's alleys and yards. Where he'd
been was compounded into a flaky Max Factor foundation
patched tissue regolith. The painter lived in the amino
acids—the chemical signals from the 100 billion neurons in
the brain. How I saw the painter was in his neural

energies and the light ups in his eyes. His personality glittered intermittently in impulse surges like a Van Cleef & Arpels window.

'Death eats you like a snake'
          he'd say
his way, the camp an ermine drawl,
'and I'm three quarters down its throat'
a rainbow boa iridescent
          as a glitter ball,
blue diamonds was how I imagined it
          blue as his Jermyn Street
Turnbull & Asser Viagra blue shirts
Egyptian cotton with Purl buttonholes
3 button cuffs or sapphire YSL:
'Age is the venom we metabolise
          the toxic squirt
like poisonous toothpaste in the arteries
          that green
it's like asparagus—poison colours
are a subtext to my palette

a depth tone, what's inside the paint,
behind the texture that you see
managed by pigment. Look for black in black
          and you find grey,
the blond boy slung on the railings today
          he's who? he's playing gay,
too fidgety, he attaches to skirts,
          I want a pink that's Campari,
(you always find them out that way),
a hot cerise, a cup cake icing pink—
          something like crushed strawberry
or the pit of a cherry stone, a pink
that mixes carbons in a red window
          over West London 6pm
February, a cherry blossom storm
of egg-whisked cumulus, carnation pink
or pouty shocking pink camellia,
          I'll never get it right

against my blue, not quite ultramarine
but never copied, more a blue that you
call imaginary blue, the best colours
          are always make up, like peacock,
or night clubbing, a smear of smudgy green
that's almost charcoal, impacted glitter
bringing up density, you don't find paint
          with the attention to detail
you get in Mac, their Russian Red Lipstick's
the intense glamour red I've never got,
a Hollywood tempo, but mixed down to
a tissue residue—you're skinnier
          than Mick Jagger, I painted him
imagining his cock was in my throat
          the snake again you see; the loop
I said that's hardwired to neurology.
          It's burning nerve that keeps me thin,
I try to write like a Jimmy Page chord
a stratospheric climb out piloted
by fuel-injected adrenalin, loud rock,
          the radar set on altered state
activities, brainwave patterns spiked up
to clip the signals, I want something new
that mixes glucose with wonk energies
and shape-shifts words into guitar figures
that rock—I'd spike a vein
rather than write into normality,
Brit lit is coloured brainfade grey, the grey
of heavy industry or river rain
pixellating the South Bank on Sunday
a grainy grey on grey on grey on grey.
          I'd like to teleport
my writing neurology to a receiving gate
somewhere out there in the blue galaxy
my data compressed into space travel,
          that's me the alien
working as a Dilly escort. 'Marty's
clean disappeared', he said,' he had the look
as natural, a mean teen on the run,

hair as I like it straight from Jimmy Dean
the gold earring a rent boy's hollow sun,
        I keep on thinking he's the one
who's fused in me as the obsessive look
I live with like addiction, it's a drug
so acute it still fires me up to paint
like someone reversed back to seventeen
and looking out for the one face, my own?—
        as I imagined it, tissue
morphed angular cheeks lifted on the bone
like Elvis, John Stephen or Jimmy Dean,
the best looking men in my life, you know
the difference between blue, pink and green,
        nobody ever gets it right
except below the stairs, sometimes the rain
is all we've got out looking for a boy,
a slow impacting moody density
like swallowing a soluble aspirin
or ibrufin, the effervescent plume
        is like chemical orgasm,
but Marty, Kenny, Johnny won't be back
the same again, they're like my afternoons
        empty of meaning, but the pain
I rub like broken glass in a pocket,
won't ever let up. Mostly Soho's dead,
the yards, the alleys, and I need a red
to hang in up of blue and pink, so volatile
it's a traffic light red or raspberry tart
as a dessert, I use vermilion
        on the side of geranium
or ruby, someone told me Johnny's dead
at seventeen, he overdosed at Kennington
in a friend's flat, 30 heroin jacks,
I'd like to paint him, I've got a photo
and stand the study against the meat rack's
infamous sarcophagus.' I'm the same
I'd blue tack poems to the railings there
rather than publish them, immediate, hot,
like downloads, give poetry to the street

as something poppy that connects
with psychoactive molecules, a beat
that puts a hook in imagery, the line's
turned in on itself as too literary
we need to free it up
with dialect, song lyric, palare,
graffiti to bash its fuckedness quotient
into a new flavour, give it a name
as something that's moved on from poetry
but still attaches to
its ambience. It's like our pink and blue
the mix never comes right. Before he died
Johnny read bits of your gift, the Sonnets
gummed with KY, maybe he took a phrase
as energy into his suicide,
you never know where a line ends or why
it means something they're hung up on inside
as a cell frequency. I only write
because nobody uses things I do
in poetry in getting into weird
or breaking with taboo,
I'm born to lose and happier that way
and started here like you on the railings
looking out at the world to meet the man
perfect for me as doing purple piss
into a rainbow coloured stream.
Your money helps to keep me clean
of strangers and liberate what I write
into the instant death of poetry,
a starburst of words into a condom.
At least I've thrown some shapes
to those who care, like the first time I heard
Marc Almond's voice and found inside its tone
a correlative suffering, a blue
inflection touching me so deep down I
could use his voice as a stairway to rainy Soho,
St Anne's Court, Green Court, Brewer, Wardour Street,
networking arteries for broken hearts
and eyes full of blue and ruby sequins.

It lives in me as resources, a pull
        into its vocal gravity
that opens gateways in my poetry,
'Sleaze', 'You Have', 'Stories of Johnny', a pop
integrated into a time and place
relocated to a memory zone
that shifts like stars leaving the galaxy.
        I haven't any place
for history, only what's in my face
when optimal surges of energy
excite the need to write. Marc's voice textures
some find in me like the smart accidents
firing up poetry—sci-fi makeup,
        a donut's wobble,
the nylon tag escaped a cerise string,
a bar mat stating I'm out with a Fag,
a raisin's downturned eye in a pancake
        the weird in almost everything
that comes up laterally. 'Marty' he said,
'did me like Peter Lacy, chained me up
and walked me round the room and thrashed me hard
        like I was locked into a yard
at Shad Thames, nothing personal, just hate
conditioned to a fetish, a complex
of cold energies up for shattering,
        I took it all the way obsessed
by finding inspiration in the pain
like a freak diamond bigger than the sun
exploding as the visionary contents
of what I'd done. I'd sometimes mix the blood
into my paint as a texturing thing
        to make red sing to olive green
and sink a deeper contemplative mood
in black lapsed into charcoal grey, a tone
        nobody ever quite achieves,
too grey, too black, the sexual undertones
tucked in. The market never knows my blood,
my haemoglobins soak in the pigment
        from being bashed across the floor

in a paint-detonated mews. I drink
not to forget but to remember pain
with alchohol's subjective clarity
and never sleep. I've come to fit that space
          so deeply I'm the contents poured
into the glass. I'm into TRTs
(tattooed rough trade) pulled from the London docks
          and used to take a chrome-buffed hearse
a friend drove as a fetish to Wapping
          and lick the sweat like diamond dust
off pectorals, I like to taste physique
          as a signature on my tongue,
an epidermal groove that feeds my art,
and sometimes love comes up in violent sex
the twisted moment of a head thrown back,
a liquid incandescence that breaks down
          resistant energies, it's what
I've only known with trade, a shattering
emotional cyclone condensed into eyes
letting go of their sex at orgasm,
the masculine exploding like a flower
          a popped morning glory
the blue concealing pink, something like that,
a transient recognition same sex stuff
by dissolving opposites makes it new
          each time, reinvents the moment
that makes straights curious, a foggy day
back of a yard at Shad Thames, a docker's
grey eyes reflected in the green water,
I knew for ten minutes the only love
          I've ever known, a pitched intensity
in which a lifetime came up like a drug
with someone accidental off a crane,
the rain starting with the meltdown into
coming, both knowing we'd never again
relive the scorched hurting intensity
          of what we shared, the river's lick
increasing with the tide, a pearl-grey pool
frothing ten metres away, London grey,

flat, chemical, and Ray now linked to me
indomitably, I held him from behind
with a velocity
like steering a car, his eyes glittering
with stars and optimal testosterone,
the city's towers leaning in
like yogic concrete, I was in so deep
separation brought immediate hate,
a dangerous, twitchy, psycho, B-side flip
to guilt, self-hatred and a level shame
compounded into menace, when he split
my lip I tasted blood back of my throat
like the river had forced on in
out of the city's networked undertow
and congealed there. He hit me once again
so hard I didn't feel a thing, then wrapped
his T-shirt round the wound before
disappearing back into a warehouse
a light on there like an abandoned sun
an orange planet from which he'd evolved
to rip my face. I washed up and cabbed back
one eye the red and indigo
of an exploded magenta tulip
and got the colour studying a mirror
to paint the lesion and the scar tissue
that beat out navy blue, a wound response
that kept the docker near
each time I consulted the raw crater
as the impacted site his knuckles bled,
I never suffer shock, the alcohol
cushions me like a wall. 'I write' I said
for sheer compression, it's a quantum thing
the attraction of images
that pull in different space-times, but co-exist
through imagination as dominant
long-range correlation of particles.
Literature's for civil servants, the grey
de facto heteros narrowing
experience to a blocked artery,

no imagery, no feeling for the real,
no psychotic juices, no peacock glow
        in the verbal rainbow,
it's only gay writers retrieve detail
from edginess and make it stick. I've found
most inspiration in the type I meet
random, opportunistic accidents
        in freefall, it's like that
the outlaw signature written in me
and coded into the hot pink flavour
of my ramped up street optimised poetry.
You gotta move and make the current move
        to get a reader, point cells up
until they're capped, it's how we remember
an image from the clutter of grey stuff
that's instantly dispersed. You paint to morph
acute self-perception at crisis point
        into atrocity, the face
in catastrophic mutation into
genocidal fuckedness, the meeting between
neurobiology and a czar's 4x4
fortress—I write like shooting film, connect
with neural terror, riff the imagery
        into a force impact
and couldn't care, I couldn't care a fuck:
poets are a die-off species, a strain
of retrovirus ejaculating bad luck.
I write in Soho, get its energy
        into my cells, I can't let go
the fact that I used the railings, no one knew,
I had to feed a line vegan protein
and helium uplift, had to have money
to keep from vulnerability, the cool
        black painted iron a support
to making out. I've no pretend the way
I've lived as an inspired subsidiary
to the city, just notching up a word
        to transport to its chemistry
without reuptake. Once I met a man

John, Johnny, Jon and went back to his place
in Charlotte Street, his bitty spill of pills
like coloured moons, his Chivas Regal glass
        manipulated obsessively,
an amber sun like pouring out a traffic light
jerking as meniscus: he burst into tears
of sexual failure and paid me to stay
and help him cry out on a black sofa,
        his shattering like rain
after the slow stacking of cumulus
over a sticky explosive West End,
I throwing lights on in his pain, his shirt
wrecked by confused emotion and he slept
        20 minutes on my chest
as a blackout respite from confusion.

What you see becomes what you see
the faces in me , names, numbers, the fog
smoky like blue candyfloss, you Francis
crumpled by introspective clarity
        you suit so sharp it hurt
because nobody noticed. Death was what
we spoke of, losing it all and winning
by de-selection—you bought me roses
and stamped a dark red one into the floor
as a reminder of ephemeral
phenomena we neither win nor lose
but keep as trashed perishable beauty.
        Another man opened the door
on a subterranean complex, black stairs
to a basement—I wouldn't follow there
in Vauxhall by the river's grungy pull
into a marzipan-coloured green pool.
He'd made the basement out a gallery
        of rent boy photos, marked the dead
with red crosses and their obituaries
as clippings—he'd been through the lot as rent
without compassion, shot up crystal meth
under the arches, missing person photos
        tacked up on the walls,

I got out sniffing a loner psycho
and made a taxi back over the river,
running scared in myself, a beady rain
drops fat as olives studding the windscreen,
        the shower's uptake like my own
in transition across the city's zones,
a blinding river silver shattering
over criminal Whitehall. We met four years
Francis and me under the city
tilting our visions like glasses of wine
collisionally, desperately at the walls.
        Knowing nothing survives
and art's like depleted testosterone,
traces hand on a smear a loaded line
with some hormonal whack, the rest blackouts
        into anonymity—
I don't remember what I did or wrote yesterday
its optimal juice turned meaningless now
unless a friend or lover finds in it
retrievable diamond dust imagery,
        a poem to me's just a hit
like sex or drugs—I don't recall a word
because the next poem displaces it,
it's like addiction, the acute habit
fed to suppress withdrawal. I couldn't care.
I've done just what I wanted to written
so wide of my ratpack contemporaries
        I'm on my own, so singular,
my education Piccadilly rent.
I've spiked poetry like a cobalt vein
into a sci-fi speed of light energy
distillation of what's glam in my time—
        Gem's birthday today from Wild Bunch,
I buy her red, yellow and bottle green
eyeshadows from Screen, coruscating dust
for facial poetry, a makeup anthology
I study as my street alchemy
        the way to write is look
at eye makeup detail not poetry

that last refuge of the pedestrian
most failed novelists turn to poetry
        and fuck it up proportionate
to desert island insularity
no drug can shift, no hallucinogen
convert into imaginative chemistry.
I've never spared myself, just gone for it
whatever I make into imagery
like a lyrical Swarovski, a burst
        of aqua in a foggy sky,
of cerise in a cherry pit, a squirt
of scarlet in the words coming up shine
        at pressure of my hand.
I like the proto-punk Elizabethans,
hard drinking, irreverent renegades
who slashed alcohol into a fine-tuned verse
for creatonin and who clashed in streets
        with rivals, Marlowe in Hog Lane
viciously using stick or Shakespeare drunk
needing a paramedic on the floor
of a Southwark bar, the river again
the colour of a martini cocktail
        twisting into a sonnet's groove
like alcoholic poisoning, the way
they wrote then, couldn't care and got it right
without edit. I used the street like that,
wrote standing up to get the dynamic
        of West End hostility
poetry as in the face irritant,
now I write outside cafes soaked in CO2
and couldn't care—poetry's graffiti—

an atomized spray gunned across a wall,
it holds a moment and grows oxidised
like wiring to a Boeing urinal,
        the uric acid corrosive
to bringing down the plane. I met a man,
ah, ha, a man slung over the railings
who said, 'you'll buy back one day what you sell,

looks when you lose them
in somebody else. That's why I'm here
and pay for what I've lost and see in you',
slim, 49?, purple cashmere V-neck,
professional, taciturn, an Earls Court type,
BMW garaged under Brewer Street,
gold bracelet thin as a spaghetti strand,
a man in his time
and no other's, all his experience
limited to genes, amino acids,
nucleotides, cellular respiration,
blood pressure like a scarlet traffic light,
facts that he couldn't get beyond
like running up against the wall that poetry
gets through by atomizing thought
into imagination—he was there—
Philip and I was hanging out
for poetry in skintight jeans, nobody normal
should approach this weird art unless you fit
a black thong like a sonnet and give up
pretensions to be a poet
an make orgasm into your epic line,
I couldn't care, only about the few
who had the gift inside them not for power
but to make the sparky image shine,

John Wieners, Jack Spicer, Robert Duncan, Jimmy
Schuyler, Lee Harwood and John Ashbery,
image manipulators, and the few
with Thom Gunn I ever remember
as anything in my glucose response
to instant hits and John Carter's
'Piccadilly Persona', the best poem
ever sent to me about rent
(Published by JTC Books PO Box 2422
(Reading R6 30 4FL
ISBN: 0-952-8000-0-4)
a black diamond gritty crafted sequence
the hurt coded into bravura

        like a 1980s Marlowe
head full of 'Tainted Love' as soundtrack
to dirty money—watermark tattoos
inked on epidermal grime, a ruby-
coloured glass ring gifted by a friend
        a sullen twinkling token
like a poem at the groin. Back of St Giles
the atrium to Centre Point, the dark
aura of the parish mixed with carbons,
nitrogen dioxide, the place psychotic,
        I hang out in a café there
and read my poems—Francis Bacon took a slash
side of the church   (a Bacon piss palette)
steaming into uric vapour, he knew
the outlawed homeless and the mad came there
and collected them as his entourage
        for dinner at Wheelers
that navy blue night, methadone users,
meths jitterers, schizos chemically coshed,
        the damaged in the city's brain
unplugged from its neurons, parallel lives
        shunted by paramilitary 4x4s
into the kerbs.
                Francis on colour—
'it's the agitated texture, blotchiness
roughed by corduroy, cashmere, scumbled,
dragged, knuckled into DNA contour,
torque, skewed, a biological impasto,
        violent pasta sauce reds, volatile
orange, fetched up on a wall or door
for grainier incision: paint's like scar tissue
it needs to leave a fingerprint, a hook
        that bites me when I'm hungover
and keeps upping tone on reality
like a red sunrise in a bottle
of Veuve Clicquot popped
for breakfast in the ruins: greens go dark
like poison, septicaemia
trawling through the blood—a green that's near black

like a blue near black, but distinctive
for how it fine-tunes green as top note
better than cobalt.' And me I don't care
          about poetry at all,
I write it as a subversive quotient
to restoring imagination as Dulux
paint gunned over reality
or spraycanned on a wall
as a virulent turquoise signature.

Poetry's a careerist cell, its operatives
          imaginatively dead
as Tiptree strawberry jam, their brainfade cells
unresponsive even to LSD
or any spiked hallucinogen,
it's mostly formulaic writing-class
limitations.   (I mean Brit poetry).
                    Once at Bankside pier

slumped in the riverbus, the sunset bleed
like tubed ketchup, tracking to Waterloo,
I met a man, ah ha, another man,
the water grey as Wrigley's spearmint gum
the undertow electrified like track
          I met a man whose poetry
was palare (polari)
a gay slang language, a vocabulary
so chippy with underworld dialect,
theatre-speak, river-speak, a compound
of the city's East/West brain hemispheres
caught in a glottal streetwise drawl
like the pink lining to a suit jacket
          a Turkish Delight pink you only see
in flicker hints of a lifted vent—
'You're bona vada' he said, 'I'm East,
the Brown family, you got a bubble-butt,
used to be a strollers omee
          joshed up like a duchess

full of billingsgate. You wanna bit of hard
I'll show ya, the name's Josh, I've got a cartzo
like you've never seen', the water ripping by
with bits of green sky towards Waterloo
        the river's frontage real estate
built up as 3 million a floor. The Waste Land
21st century, with its Whitehall czars
clammy with high cholesterol, the light
        focused like spot gold shares
on Peninsula Heights, a rubbled beach
searched by the sticky city tide, my friend
Bill Franks up on the second floor at 10
        in a strawberry Jaeger jumper,
I need him there the way I need
habituated Valium in my cells
or poems by John Wieners. A friend's
a way of keeping focus in a life
even by familiarizing an address,
storing a number. Bill's chrysanthemums
sent as a gift shook up blue December,
pink chrysanthemums , spiky, rayed-out stars
frosty as an ironed shirt. (Japanese),
        it's always a stand out detail
survives as a neuronal accident,
Bill answering the door with 40 years
love for a man (John Stephen) in his eyes
together with the river's green sparkle,
their creation the 1960s look
        for men, singular proponents
of the only look, I see
John in Bill's eyes, so too the book
I've written on them, an orange uplift
in grey sky ideologies—
a fashion gene they injected in me
as enthused energy to recreate
their story as saints of Carnaby Street's
red brick recessed barrio—they were there
        and Bill's still there, my book's
the quantum leap between the two,

a polarising star. The river turns
mid-stream into conflicting energies
        like a hand clap, a push
and opposition, like the river drowned
in a bottle green whirlpool with the sun
sucked under like red glycerine—
London doesn't belong to anyone
        we're facts passing through like rogue genes
as disinformation. Bill's kitchened now
with Jaffa cakes and beginnings of tea,
        a white jumper tubed over jeans,
solicitous, and just the brightest light
come up and round him, it's a diamond tray
converted into psychic energy
        a compound brilliance I see
as sparkle, those accelerating stars
glittering as his personality,
as inimitably individually Bill
        this transparent blue October day,
the flat sighting the river, it's our lives
connect this moment over Jaffa cakes—
54 mm in diameter, a sponge cake base,
orange flavoured jelly like a UFO
        diameter 38 mm,
the chocolate seducing the orange jam
into a McVitie's bite—
                                Bacon on purple—

'It needs a third primary in the mix
as green as contributive to red and blue
        to get an edge on magenta
or violet—purple's a draggy blue
a Vauxhall Tavern mood pigment,
a hot and cool dissolve, I get it right,
it's eggplant not inkplant, an up-downer,
        dominant, not lavender
that drags with blue or deeper indigo,
purple's like an elephant's death
        a withdrawal into still thunder

like an aircraft hanger. It's crushed figs
and car paint better than the lot
purple cellulose—I do purple best
an update on Velázquez, Liz Taylor's
eye makeup in Cleopatra, how to lift
tone out of purple without ramping up
its gravity, beetroot's too red
unless you imagine it bluer-red
coming up purple. And purple broccoli
it's too close to maroon. Get purple right
and you get black, fucking Velázquez black
like the bottom of a stairwell
or the Thames—I mean I mix it drunk
it's Dean Street purple, metabolised booze
molecularised in paint. Purple's a fight
you have to beat it black and blue
to make it happen right
it's the colour compressed in a boxing glove
or the hex in a criminal tattoo,
a nipple or a fuchsia bud,
the idea of a colour that resists
interpretation, purple's an idea
not a tonal reality
like a magnolia's plashy tongue, or Fatou's
toes painted as a signalling keyboard.
I met a man, ah, ha, another man
at the City of Québec, Marble Arch,
(The Elephant's Graveyard), his eyes mixed gin
with loneliness into a no-colour
like a glass of water seen neutral blue,
a man who'd selected a year in which to live
and stay there in a resistant space-time,
his mother alive, his music
the internalised soundtrack to his space—
blues he said, blue devils in R&B,
and in his head a black knitted square end tie,
a Hardy Amies
looped like a blunt-headed snake
over a pink shirt, a bottle of Cutty Sark,

the time exactly 7 p.m.,
his mother out, the light projected gold
as an anthology of bits
shot as hot photons from the galaxy,
he let me into that in that far into the fine-tuned
neural networks protecting his MySpace
the lazy evening like an orange cat
whatever year it was that kept him there
still re-evaluating its contents
as though it was his present not the past
as though the tie still awaited the shirt
the black knot tight
as bunched silk given a black patterned glaze.

He took me back to Sussex Square, a flat
in which the ceiling was a strawberry cake,
the floor a marble thunderstorm, the shirt
and tie recreated on the bed
as a fixated fetish, pink and black
unworn separates confected in his head
to the same calibration keeps a thought
in place a lifetime (DNA
methylation—methyl chemical caps),
the sex dissociated like he had
orgasm in another time, a space
so far removed from Sussex Square, he shot
in Bangkok, Berlin or Dubai
connecting with an attached fantasy
in opalescent beads like snail glitter
over his navel, a handjob
for which he paid fifty, my writing hand
worth fifty and a taxi back
to Regents Park, the moon beach curved façade
to Park Crescent—poetry paid by sex
I couldn't care—the line is gold
and kicks in—I do poetry
so much better than my contemporaries
because it's so imaginatively immediate.
Poets get paid in rain,

or turquoise sequins I smack in the air
when reading at First Out—the basement dark
for throwing shapes from poetry,
sequins as substitute for salary
          as starbursts under a spotlight
filtering lapis lazuli—that's me
I couldn't care a fuck for poetry
          that's mainstream, I'm an addict
for imagery only—OD on it—
like mixing heroin with helium.
I met a man, ah, ha, another man,
          a suit—I mean a charcoal grey
who took me lunches, I was 120 lbs
of fine-tuned poetry, my hand
          turning gold from a tricky wrist
like water poured into whiskey,
          I had a subtle twist
that brought this man off and I never ate
just drank his wine, a Chablis or Sancerre,
a Château Margaux, a St Julien
the colour of wine poured in a black bra
          and fingered on a nipple,
an areola plum or indigo or black,
I'd keep him on delay like finger stops
played on the frenum until he came
as starburst in a rubber,
my hand that turned poems got rich by turns
of sensation—money to write and play
and hang out afternoons at the Dilly
          writing poems on the railings
as a street signature.

                                        Bacon on orange—
'don't pretend it's red or yellow,
it's programmed for an explosive tone,
a solar epicentre, buy Jaffas
and stamp on them in biker boots, it's violent
if you get it live, the revs full-on
like a colour assault. I got it right

mixed on a wall in 1949
my Velázquez rehash, all screaming hybrids,
orange accelerated in a rush
as pure sensation—I paint to avoid
narrative, the texture's like a haemorrhage,
a clotting that pulls back on linear
development by words, the line
looking to link with another.
Orange to me is like a fist
slammed into green or black or blue,
a contentious diagram, more a slash
of vitamins into the mix,
I keep it livid. It's the afterglow
to sex shot through with hangover,
as orange neon in the brain.
My palette's urban, I don't do sunsets
like a galactic juicer, I shrink space
to where we live, a room
as the turbulent arena
in which we encounter most everything.
Orange is more off-mood than red.
Orange attracts purple, nobody wears
orange with any style, it sucks,
but toned up ripping into black
I get it so acute it hurts to look.
Orange is awkward, it's so loud
it's like it's miked into an attitude.
You get it sometimes in an egg,
in the raw moment when it starts to cook
with viscous cholesterol, aggressive yolk
that orgasms into the pan—'

I met a man, ah ha, another man
outside Boots on a hazy afternoon
          brown-eyed Bill who looked my way
and turned away furtively, came on back
affirmatively, it was in his look
the need to bring his loneliness back home
to mother, skinny, 50+

exec, green candy-striped Brooks Brothers button-
down, (poets always lack clothes
details, my grey contemporaries)
hardwired features, speech like an apple bite
of punchy clarity, Canali suit
3-button charcoal with flat front trousers.
a man used to Bentley's and the Ivy
for lunches that were oystery
with slippery rainbows, it was in the crisp
expensive tone, the voice supported by money,
the need expressed like a contract,
an illegal same-sex pick-up,
the softness underneath like a pink dye
colour of a fifty pound note,
only he wasn't sure where, the hotel
notoriously monitored, downstairs
dangerous as pulling a gun,
his place in Cadogan Square, hesitant,
I didn't know the man, but that's not the deal
to eat for poetry,
the taxi over to Chelsea, the crowds
like footage, the day turned London rainy
big city grey, like the sky was the sea,
and I dissociated, quizzical,
black cashmere jumper, black skinny jeans
dismissing him, something about the voice
caught in my nerves, a psychopathic twist
of depersonalised cool.
I left him with the cab and walked away,
his eyes bulleting my retreat
through pessimistically uplifting rain—
Bacon, 'I'm optimistic about nothing'
and picked up later, it was the highlights
won me over, the stand out blond
like sunlight worked into black hair, sleepers
in either ear, a flat in Half Moon Street
so local it was a heartbeat
away—I never thought I'd do these things
for poetry, because nobody cares

in poetry if poets die, it's all
an asphyxiating corrupt coterie
          of what Francis called 'cannibals
without imagination'—orange smacks
the viewer with a blood-hot slap, an optimal
bloody mary—red exhilaration,
a red acceleration through yellow
to fuck you orange. It's the solar core
squeezed cold out of a tube, but got blood-hot
by my impacted impetus. Coronal orange
like betacaritone or the fire glow
round the galaxy's ruby-red core.
I met a man ah, ha, another man
          my writing hand an investment
in underworld shares, washed Dilly money,
          dollars printed by London light—
and written on by poetry, the need
I had to write so unconditional
it never allowed for alternative
in anything—the line dusted by foundation,
rain, light pollution, fine particles, chance,
          ultraviolet radiation,
blood tracking from a finger, sticky leak
congealing in Pentel, a mauve U-turn
fingerprinted into a grainy smear.
I met so many strangers in that way
          the poem in me full of city sky
bluely reflected from a Harrods floor,
a West End poem with its dialect
          as fast as a pop single
and as transient. Rent gets its power
from turning men away, I put them down
in numbers, like I couldn't care
for what they offered, money in their come
          like rhinestones twinkling on a sleeve,
demoted their individuality
by look, the hurt went deep with some,
as part of an intuitive exchange,
men sent off namelessly into the crowd

that never stops—the desperate ones
who go back downstairs to the underground
and the whining discourse of tubes
hardwired into the city's diaphragm—

Bacon on black—
'It needs to be differentiable from blue,
a no-colour signifier
like a lights out in the tube.
Black's more a state than mood,
it's palpable even in a Rothko
where there's no signature texture in paint,
no roughage like my track marks in pigment,
my tyre treads of explosive energy
worked into a resistance to settle,
a spiky, edgy, worked over attack.
Black's
central issue to all serious theme,
you get with it what you suggest—it's death
and what goes on back of colour,
even a black cab alters traffic mood
by being black
under a rainy sky. Black pulls you in
to its interior:' (I broke off writing
to have a Kitkat here and read a text
from Wakako: Jeremy how are you?
I send you purple power from Paris
I miss you and I'm blue):
and Bacon, 'black argues significance
by attracting all colours by contrast,
black paint's the best radiative cooling,
it's also ultraviolet
and absorbs looking like it absorbs light,
it's best seen reflecting on a black eye.'
The darkest material on earth's
created by carbon nanotubes stood on end
a scientific black
reflecting only .045 percent of light.

A Bacon black's a tragedy

rehearsed in a living-room, a queer black
with bitchy pull into a black context,
a fist fight with George Dyer in a sack.
        Black's complex in its mixed pigments,
he never told me black was dark matter
totalling most of the black universe
beyond the atmosphere, dirt and glitter,
        and the black railings at the Dilly
flaking paint into every rent boy's palm
        as a removable tattoo,
the bits comprising duration—I came and went
as transient head-turning
stunning duplicitous rent.
I couldn't care, I'll die as a failure
up against it all, but for poetry
        as all I've got and done
unsparingly—given every moment
        to something that's original
and bleeds defiance like a chemical
into brain chemistry.
                        Selling myself
as only way out of routine, a singular
application to poetry: today
at Peter's house, 20 Holland Park Avenue
(the house a soap-blue almost lavender)
I told him what I'd done—the Russian fridge
a white psychotic slab in the corner
of the basement kitchen, Peter's fry up
spitting like heating a Pollock painting
in an oiled steering wheel sized frying pan,
the egg and tomato collisional
        in an auroral clash
of fatty primaries, Peter's relapse
into popping grease and a ruined pan
        his 15 stone to my nine
working for poetry—the rooms' cryopreserved
with family gunk, nothing and everything
fixed immovably into place.
I tell Peter Shakespeare paid for sex

punter or rent it's all the same
and none of his deferential biographers
have ever raised the idea of orgasm,
          its price and availability
to his alcoholic testosterone
and how he fucked boys—it's in the sonnets—
his juice 100% poetry,
like me he wrote with nothing else to do,
and no micro-thin Kimono condom.
Round the back of St Giles Church
Shakespeare and Marlowe came together in fog,
it's in my hallucinated novel *The Grid*
ISBN 978-0-7206-1303-2 (Peter Owen)
and in their shocking reality,
disease, desire, lawless punk outlaws
          using a blade or stick
to turn a trick.
                                        Peter's magenta splashed
Thai silk shirt detonates purple roses
as pattern on a turquoise base,
a Bangkok shirt that's a tropical blast
in London W11, every room
blocked with the books he's published the logo
PO, endemic signature
to stand out prose, the sort that's poetry
without the need to advertise.
A house that's dusted, re-regulated,
a lowlight interior, every fixture
obsessed over, secured in place
          by mental polymer,
a house so often home to my breakdowns
a sanctuary when shattered into bits
and seeing things, hallucinated pulls
of scary imagery—I couldn't go outside
          for fear of being locked up, coshed
by toxic psychiatry, dense plane trees
          so green outside, a jungle green
swimming above the avenue like fish,
a surge of breeze in photosynthesis,

and opposite, I'd walk up there,
Hillsleigh Rd, No 19a,
Anna Kavan's for a decade,
a white house like the Chinese heroin
she shot into a network of popped veins
writing Ice like visionary molecules
frozen into glacial imagery
a blue glow as the surround sound
on everything—dopamine poetry
blazingly cold emeralds and sapphires
tooled by her fine-tuned freebasing
the drug into deacetylated 6—
monoacetylmorphine (6-MAM)
and chilling in the histamine release
to writing, the drug binding to
u-opioid receptors and in turn
to Anna's writing chemistry,
the jabs she gets off riffy accelerated
energy out of heroin dust
like a car blasting out of sand.
Anna in her reclining leopardskin lounger,
hair dyed Warhol sunlight platinum
a silk dress bagged from Harrods
for the purchase thrill, the attitude
of an implacable diva, her cool
so focused it could freeze
like cryopreservatives, her ODs
so many they were trial obituaries
for the final whiteout—
I wrote my book
on her, Stranger On Earth,
partly sitting outside her house, spring showers
detonating the torchy chestnut
flowers, and a purple lippy magnolia
starting to shatter into cerise silk
and got the feeling and the look
of Anna's alien pathology,
her smacked-out rented depression
the opposition that she got above

to work with no advance and no
PR, just habit, like another drug,
novels that only reached a cult
but keep on going, spiky dystopian things
that flare into poetry
like a humming bird opening ruby wings
inside a dusty lily.

There's no reward, a local readership
of friends—Peter standing in the kitchen
in a split dressing gown, sunlight collecting
into a photon honey jar
of amber light sculptures—'She was a snake
in jewels, a lying bitch, but great
in a frosty drugged way, remote, too chilled
to ever get to know, the drug
was the divisive, she would leave the room
to inject her reality
and pick at chocolates on the bed, sweet tooth
and smack, clean private drugs.'
Peter after twenty glasses of wine,
fridge-fat, skewed, patting a glazed pound
Fortnum's rich fruit cake, coaxing out cherries
before the disappearing act,
the thing digested like a snake.
Anna was thin as light arrived
from the helical galaxy, size zero,
(this is her debut in a poem)
the spotlight on her which she can't contest
40 years after her terminal OD
fatty mitochondria
of the heart—degenerate H damage
to her arteries :
(I exited the poem here
went out to Shu Uemura—Seven Dials
to view his silicone-coated eye colours—
poets need colours like injected vitamins
I chose for Toyoko
an orange pressed powder: Neon Sunset,

and then to Screen on Monmouth Street
for a Ben Nye LU-12 Cosmic Blue,
the two colours forming a smudged sunset
          the things I do
go back to poetry
          a valium 5 mg
as a retarded yellow sun,
store the poem in my limbic zone
like a bullet in a gun,
buy a kitkat and aqua micro-thin
          kimono condoms,
tofu for protein:
                    Anna's urn is buried
under a laurel tree back of the house
at Hillsleigh Road, incinerated molecules
compacted into a crunchy ash
I'd like to spoon into my hand   like heroin
to shoot into the 21st century,
Keith Richards snorted his father's ashes
as sinewy cocaine,
and today the monochrome monosyllabic
London rain opens polka dot patterns
over the Dilly, Hillsleigh Road, 20 Holland Park Ave
and my life soundtracked by London rain
signatured into my poetry,
all those nights listening out to its discourse,
its iambic diary in my nerves
          come up to sustain
that colours in its moving on
          like a dollop of 24 carat gold
flashed into its constituents.
I met a man, ah ha, another man,
          on the Piccadilly concourse,
someone who kept reinventing himself,
his nervous rush settling down like a drink
          hitting the abdomen
as a chemical shooting star.   Charley
(Charlie), cornered grey eyes, his thoughts downturned,
          he spoke into himself not up

into the next level, an oranger
variant of himself, the meeting's split-
second, instinctual on both parts,
          you read a person's type or let
them go back to the underground, afraid
the mismatch was a damage commentary
on both, no matter how casual
          the encounter, I've seen them all
the punter coterie, the up and down
          staring me down against the wall
as though I had no personality
          but sex, no gunning accelerated
impulsive contract with weird poetry
as my identity. Lack of money
          took me to the railings a time
to live off crime—I had no other way
          and Charley (Charlie) was a fact
cohering from the fast indifferent crowd,
white jumper, lived-in chinos, strawberry voice,
          hair split like sunlight and shadow,
a man sold on the danger in his need
to aberration: hurt had corrupted
          like a bruise inside his voice,
he wanted a café first, then his flat
as assignation, I could see the sweat
          collecting as a commentary
of sticky apprehension—the dead air
          smelling of the tube's clinical
efficiency, and Piccadilly Line
anonymity—and he went for it
          the small café on Denman Street
in a state of perpetual fry,
a choked greasy London vernacular
of popping cholesterol, his tan wallet
          observably crammed with plastic,
a violet sleepless hoop beneath each eye,
taupe birthmark like a jellyfish
          mapped under the left ear, burn mark
nicked on the lower lip, off-white hand knit

polo, graphite chinos, distressed finish,
Charley (Charlie) he only wanted head
and a consolatory hour,
the city power-pointed in his cock
with big gonadal revs like dollars,
ex-public school, impersonal sex,
self-consciously angled across the bed,
his shape reminding me of loneliness
in white Burlingtons stuffed full of money
I had to retrieve (his fetish)
while coaxing him towards inhibited
orgasm like a lava lamp
ballooned in a coral rubber teat.

(I took another break here, listened to
Dusty Springfield finding a gradient
drenched in saturated colours, deep blues
like Bacon's abraded impasto,
took a slug of hexy Cutty Sark, her voice
rivered into my arteries,
fired off emails, went to Camden Market
to pick up designer jackets,
I have a rail of seventy, bussed in
to 44 Bedford Court Mansions
to my favourite orange sunshine kitchen
Alan's high-rise of spilled papers,
erotic drawings, stories, music scores,
polythene bags like body bags
of rent boy photos all over Soho
isolated into his shoot
as missing persons, disinformation
heaped on the kitchen table as outlaws
who sold the only thing they had
a skinny habituated body,
Alan gave me the blueberries and nuts
he'd stolen from his local Sainsbury's
part of a criminal fetish
to shoplift as a surge of energy
against capitalist ethic.

I left Alan and read my Mac receipt

as impromptu poetry:
773602137138 (4) Small Eyeshadow Clarity
9.79x1 9.79
Served by Tomoko
Ref 65851-3-58015 VPM
19/12/2008 18.23.31

Tomoko looked manga, her red lipstick
a glamorous lyric,
her eyes the size of black olives, her skin
like a magnolia petal,
her name a chocolate poem on the tongue,
her inclusion in poetry
a first: I kept turning her face over
walking across town, a romance
lived off a printed receipt as first steps
to poetry. In Goodwin's Place
her recreated image came so clear
I wrote her name across a wall
in Pentel as a sign, a cryptic clue
bleeding into the city's scrambled text
a purple Tomoko in a passage
back of St Martin's Lane, the secret thrill
of instant infatuation. I save
Tomoko's image neutrally
for future writing, there's no copyright
on use, poets are criminal
shape-shifters of internalised reality—
I take my subjects their poems
to add to the complicity,
poetry's like striptease with imagery,
a seamed nylon, black garter belt
doing smoke and mirrors with flesh,
a sequinned stiletto
a walk with words throwing shapes on the page
to a burlesque soundtrack
for Tomako.

A poet's A-B

means dissolving words into experience
    as one reality,
the line growing into a black-eyed saint
    of criminality—
                Bacon on paint
'All colours agree in the dark,
there's no schematics, just instinctual build
as tonal chemistry, abrade the lot,
the paint in opposition to itself
cyclonically, a green and red
in direction collision like a car crash
working to counteract velocity
by impacting head on—I still can't get
colour to do the quantum trick
and be in two places at once—a slash
of obsidian against hectic blue
demands a Ferrari red and a pink
you get in cup cakes or glossy car paint
    or cherry pits and campari
or a black-eyed pink liquorice all sort
and slapped on with my knuckled fist.'
I couldn't give a fuck for poetry—
    I see my lines as cake toppings,
sexy hard-punching bits of imagery
    like a Red Velvet chocolate sponge
dyed scarlet with Soviet frosting
(Callebaut Belgian chocolate and Nielsen-Massey vanilla)
or a wacky Elvis banana cake
with coffee-glazed butter icing
or a flirty frou frou signature cake
    pitted with raspberries and coconut—
donut style squirted with berry-clustered black jam
for sugar quotient:
    the edge of this page bleeds into
Adam Johnson who joined Aids departures
    at 28—my elegy
'Outside Foyles' recreating his blond look
and love-heart face burnt down by plague, his cells
    retro-virused from semen-banks
propagated on rainy Hampstead Heath

under the lit up orgy tree,
a blue bonfire with knotty oak antlers
and Adam facing the red glow
of flame, bareback sex, anonymity,
the brutal sweat of HIV
the morning after, volcanic fever,
a reinhabited body
morphed by undercover policing of the genes—
Adam as a thin survivor
virus-carrier Brompton cemetery
outlaw for a resistant poetry
that infiltrated through pamphlets
to weirdo off-planet outtakes like me
looking for kicks—I'm just a crimson kid
that you won't date; but Adam's line
taking its pointer from Gunn dominates
by impacted resilience,
Elizabethan muscle in its push,
the best of it coming up shine
like 'The Departure Lounge' arguably
unrivalled for dexterity
March 1992, Adam's finest,
I mean nobody gets that good
writing out of contaminated blood—

shodooby dooby dooby do—Adam
'clenching our pills,
We leave our doctors, newly diagnosed,
Think only of the virus that it kills
And how much to confide—or are composed,
Armed with a clearer knowledge as we chance
A cool controlled reaction: I recall
Profound relief, a kind of arrogance,
I had not reckoned that the sky would fall.'
The tone's so right on
metaphysical, so confrontational
and up against the wall
it's like Elizabethan pop, a hook
so sinewy it kills

if you're in the right nerve as the reader
undercover in the virus
copied into poetry an HIV transcript
lyric, different again
from straight poetry as leafy Hampstead
from neutral Piccadilly rain,
a man with incurable PCP
programmed into his writing breath
at Redcliffe Gardens, shaping out his death
by having bits of the process rhyme,
deconstructing cells as hexameters
11/2 / 92
'Dear Jeremy' I find my handwriting less clear
for some reason at 28
thanks for your generous words about my poetry
I'm Aids and virus-stamped
if I should get a book, I start to fear
I'm running out of time through whisked cement.
Your reading last night was spectacular
as a star...' December's like a green diamond
with a minus 10 glow
18 carat ice filmed over the sky,
the brutal black-holed star-gobbling galaxy
out there as dark matter,
indifferent energy, I work the line
back of St Giles, at First Out
light up time, 6pm white night lights
signalling from each table
like wax cup cakes, the drinks beginning now
to hit in and metabolise
as lift-off, lights on dimmers, the music
so dancy it's like oxygen
streaming into the cells, while I exist
like a bubble in obsidian,
a brain plugged into the universal stars
as alien intelligence
in a London bar, a glittered mirror
spatializing the floor.
Adam's as dead as Marlowe or someone

dying now as I write the word
into oblique wonk-planes tracking the sky
go places all day I don't know
with only contrails for a signature.
But Marlowe's death, he pissed in streets
adjacent to First Out, a slashed rainbow,
still fascinates like Elvis',
Monroe's, John Lennon's, Sid's or Kurt Cobain,
at swampy Deptford Creek, a slow
hand on the syrupy green tide,

it's muscle twisting with Chiltern water
and Kit there 30/5/1593
hallucinated from poetry and drink
a punkish double agent recklessly
meeting with dodgy criminals, erect
from danger, sailors, smoking pot
with blacks under the street, black tobacco
was marijuana streaming with visions
of a black eagle flying a rainbow
out of its beak over the Thames,
morphing into a black terrorist plane
shattering lit fuel through a tower
in rumbles of explosive kerosene.
Was Kit's last taste fellatio
or blood?—a spy meeting with gofer type
extortionists, Poley, Frizer, Skeres,
lowlife from London yards, faking money,
fucking in alleys, partying
with knives, burying diamonds in honey,
Frizer ripped Marlowe through the eye
through the superior orbital fissure
a direct pathway to the brain
haemorrhaging—the blade 2 inches in
puncturing the carotid artery,
metal and intracranial bleeding
severing nerves to poetry,
the body summarily under rain
stamped underground in bloody sheets,
a fact in the homicide quotient,

the contract put out by Shakespeare
to liquidate a lover and rival—

the publisher Thomas Thorpe:

I purpose to be blunt with you, & out of my dullness
to encounter you with a Dedication in the memory of
that pure Elemental with Christopher Marlow: whose
ghost of Genius is to be seen walk the Churchyard
in (at the least) three or four sheets.

Marlowe's prototypical punk disdain,
the culprit sprayed over the wall
in visceral graffiti: a big death
to little poetry, I keep
neuroimaging what he might have been,
buying a Big Purple, the sweet
shaped like a turtle shell in purple foil
38 gm of sticky hazelnut
clenched by caramel, a rogue outtake
Quality Street, Energy 789 kj/189kcal
Protein 1.9 g, Carbohydrate 23.2 g,
Sugars 19.3 g, Fat 9.8 g
Calories 191.0,
Pete Doherty brings me Big Purple,
size of a 35 mm candle light bulb
or a purple Art Deco brooch
an ostentatious splash of purple paste.
Marlowe would have pocketed Big Purple,
stolen them from J&K Food and Wine
on Charing Cross Road, so I fantasize
his eyes fixed inward on a line
turning from orange to gold metaphor
his contempt for his own poverty
spat out as diamante saliva.

Britney Spears in purple panties

What are the neural substrate at work now
juicing a poem I can't see

come up at Seven Dials, do I fit the place
        into the prefrontal cortex,
so that Gem's tall-stemmed heavy red roses
        intrude as image acquisition,
a red the colour of Saint Julien
        jam sponge and a vamp's lippy
         colouring like a love-bite.
I pilot the poem on automatic
        pocketing into disconnect
to talk to friends, do other come up things
        like shops or make black China tea
            Zheng Shan Xiao Thong
(Lapsang Souchong)—a dragon in the pot
        of calligraphic smoky steam—
and Marlowe, I've lost interest in him now
        like a face on Charing cross Road
gone underground at Leicester Square
        Tomoko in Mac Russian Red
a hint of scarlet in her hair?
        Kit will resurface in my life
as I imagine him in my changes,
        my cellular mutations, the knife
that killed him buried somewhere in debris
        compacted on the Greenwich road,
DNA traces from 1593.
        Like Elvis there are Kit sightings,
the condensed attitude inside a bar
        that morphs into a bloody eye
like a red light plugged in the room
        at Deptford on a pelting night
and in between scratchy guitar assault
        the spiky haired kid at the mike
spontaneously admits he's Kit Marlowe
        on a dopamine rush,
four-chord poetry and a purple bike
to wing it back to Shoreditch.

I met a man, ah ha, another man
brokering the Dilly concourse,

two-coloured socks, one flamingo, one black,
        Kenzo blazer, 40" fit,
Micky who worked menswear at Selfridges
        and had a trust and played a bit
cherry picking rent. His equivocal
        response, 'you must be an artist'
was always perfunctory apology
        for picking up, 'you look the part'
as though I didn't, Nicky moved like rain
        twisting in wind, a flicky head
alert to angles and potential threat,
        'your sort don't usually come here',
his hair so kept it was patisserie,
        a blueblack rococo wave
articulated above Med-blue eyes,
        his speech a set of signals
transmitted by a look, and up for it
        with cash, he peeled off a blusher pink
fifty with rehearsed audacity,
        his place a Mews off Ladbroke Grove,
a cobbled recess, orange ranunculus
        bunched compositely in a vase,
a bottle of gin on the ironing board
        a slew of rooky paperbacks
Goldfinger, Other Voices Other rooms,
        a red-eyed Naked Lunch, Burroughs
doctored by Ian Somerville, the man
        shrunk to reptilian alien
an intravenous H. Micky was in
        the Tetleys and detonating
chocolate digestives as preparatory
        to fixing nervous dialogue,
pre-sex, the money to my writing hand
        a futures contract, a James Bond
acceleration into poetry
        so based in neural happening
it jumps a century ahead, no word
        included that's a backword look
in getting there. Micky's sounds worked the room

Billy Holiday's violet tone
sipping at pain like poison on a spoon,
her heart that broken, all the bits
collected in her grainy voice, the scars
like distress in a leather sleeve—
'can't help lovin' that man of mine'
and Micky wagging out his cock,
his dopamine spiked up to apogee
stimulated opiate receptors/
endorphins like a blast of red sunshine,
bulleting his brain, what I did
was booster tricks, my tongue and fingers twinned
with sensual teasing, a slo-mo
inciter to surges of caviar
hot thunder in the coaxed scrotum,
the come so concentrated, it's a lake
forced vertically into the air
in surges. Micky chilling instantly
legs crossed like a leggy girl,
his biscuit a chocolate skinned crescent moon
blue hair flipped into a redo
and friends immediately.
Bacon on clothes—
'the look's the killer, it's a cross
between big-shouldered Miami Vice
and authentic Savile Row—Tommy Nutter
for instance, the wild child maestro
fusing London's East/West sartorial
dialect like polari
a dissolve of gangster and bohemian
no stylist ever exceeds 38"—40" chest,
shoulder to shoulder 17"
sleeves, shoulder seam to cuff 24",
base of collar to hem 29"
underarm to underarm 20"—
single breasted 4 button fastening
4 buttons per cuff (2 working)—
straight set pockets, twin rear vents,
a lining slash like a colour block,

a colour moment ripping out
in scarlet, gold, purple, Cadillac pink
or blinding juicy Californian orange.'
I never saw Bacon dress down, his style
mixed Ted, Mod, underworld dandy
into personalised panache—
a Rive Gauche blue YSL button down,
black knitted silk tie, or a splash
of blue and black coordinated stripes
matched with an aluminium shirt
set apart by selective choice, a grey
the colour of a Wapping pier,
a queer pink, the colour of pink champagne
as a footnote to a grey suit
as Frenchified Bethnal Green. Dust
or cremated ashs perfects the colour
for a grey suit?—the contamination
of dress into image—the paint soaked socks
and cashmere sweaters ribbed into
agitated pigment, the impasto
shocked up like indigo custard.
Francis made leather into a sleek skinned camp
a zippered streetwise blouson
worn with black chinos or bovver-boy jeans
hitched onto scarlet braces,
his hair dyed to accommodate the teens
he scooped off the meat rack
as the extension to himself, the look
he configurated through paint and sex
like barebacking a crocodile
or improvising tango with a bull
to wrestle paint.

'Some paint comes across directly onto the nervous system and other paint tells you the story in a long diatribe through the brain.' FB

The work-out's in the mutilated thrash,
the urban narrative he finds

in stripping faces to a side of beef
like a shark gash, the red lesion
the catastrophic pointer like a star
to who we are as basic quotient—
a Bacon rip.
I got picked up
so often, and turned down most all
as fake gold, a street currency
I didn't need, and let them fall
back in the stairwell under the city,
Dave, Robert, Johnny, Bill, Andy and Jake
as fucked up supernumeraries
part of the mortmain of ephemeral facts
condensed into the west End dirt
I didn't need, just hanging out an hour
to suck the sunlight like honey
into edgy poetry. Some afternoons
I really thought the light stood still
I occupied my time so optimally
in local space I made my own
by a defiantly resistant look
a blond purchase on reality
reading Ashbery in rushed bitty excerpts
that seemed to fit the poetry's
random sightings, its lack of a subject
like sitting down without a chair,
the thing just moving in a formless way
mapping no resolution, quirky, cute
as a stylized hair redo
a remake of the Elvis quiff
as adaptable currency,
the air pockets like crossing the data-line
above an aqua limpid sea,
the 747 jolting, the cabin air
smelling of impersonal anise
and a cold bacterial soup. Read laterally
without any care of meaning
but more as space tourism poetry's
tolerable for a few minutes

as an instantaneous altered state fix
or a dollop of J&B
to up blood temperature, but lacking blues:
'It could be a spoonful of coffee
it could be a spoonful of tea
but one little spoon of your precious love
is good enough for me'
a Willie Dixon narrative
as true as taste. The blues permeate everything
that puts beat in the blood
changing a glass button to a sapphire
a paste brooch into a ruby
a hole in the heart into a rose
a dusty hat to an affair
that wins such hooky chords it travels right
across the feeling universe
leaving most poetry cold, insular,
stupidly retrograde, frigid,
and lacking snake-piss in its recipe
to come up right in virus shells
injected into the chemistry.
Let's do it then, rewrite Shakespeare
a queer redo of a sonnet
reorganize the language not the plot
like a DJ remix
colouring the original, I couldn't care
I've no respect for history (Sonnet 101)
'What's in the brain that writing brings alive
that hasn't baby always been in you
there's nothing on the charts that seems to drive
my message home or tell you that I'm blue?
There's nothing new babe in turning a trick
and only come alive—you for a dick
and me by making poetry an event.
I'd like to think words reconstruct a face
like botox or the surgeon's tuck resists
the lived—in creases that come to replace
the youthful image that we know exists
resistantly beneath the damage done

and couldn't care and live by going on.'
I did that in the café next
Charing Cross Mansions, it took ten minutes
writing, eating, scrambling a text
and concentrating on Will, Willy, Bill
enigmatic as dark matter
that keeps galaxies from flying apart
there's 24 trillion metric tons
of dark matter between the earth and moon
like Willy's brain compact
with neural metric, boozed-up grey matter
with neurons switched on like the galaxy,
size of an iceberg lettuce, but so fast
thoughts travelled at the speed of light
with photon clarity. 'Can't help loving dat
man of mine,' he sang over breakfast
in a leopard-print trackie
his wife hexing a doll with voodoo pins
to kill the unrepentant rent
he'd made his spotty smelly bit of stuff
as a dubious scandalous event.
'I'm lonesome,
God, so lonesome,
Hear me cryin',
Baby I ain't lyin',
I'm so lonesome, got those lonesome At-
lanta Blues,
I'm so sad and lonesome, mama, don't
know what to do'—
that's Bobby Grant on rootless loneliness
I heard a boy sing in the Dilly loo
as consolation for his homeless
degradation, selling sex
to feed a state broken like guitar strings,
his blood infected by needles,
his absolute bottom working the street's
stinging lawless hostility
but reachable by a consoling blues
dusting him with the alchemy

to convert despair into scratchy song
an aching mantra done in time
to a gummed City of Westminster mirror,
a blues as blue invocation
to lyric breath climbing out like a snake
into raspy phrases, guttural
streetwise, wheezy like blues in bronchiae,
the instant unforgettable
to me and whoever absorbed those notes
as unrehearsed poetry
'I'm lonesome
God, so lonesome
Hear me cryin'
Baby I ain't lyin'
under the street, all of us there
underworld outtakes skinned of social place
the Haymarket's sunny economy
minutes away, optimistic workspace
spiking up money like helium,
meeting rooms, staffed reception,
aspidistra, achemea, crassula
greening the atrium, snouty gingers
simmering with tusked potential
like Amazonian sex, a ruby pink
under the tongue tone—invites
to global commerce. I tasted sunshine
as gold and hung out for a suit
to inject money into poetry
like respiration into St Louis blues.
'I was standing on the corner with my hat
in my hand
Standing on the corner with my hat in my hand.
Looking for a woman, didn't have a man'—
Pink Anderton, the blues fits need
as shaping poetry, the red wine
I've fuelled into my arteries
the buried sun in a Château du Paradis
fermented sunlight sourced
to redden out the galaxy

and be converted back to poetry
as measure of galactic
industry. A red Bordeaux energy
whacked through my neurochemistry
writing these words at First Out, Lorena
and Malcolm entering the phrase
I pit like an olive to come up right
as holding good against the pack
who squeeze me out of credibility.
'Why don't you do right?'
as Billie sings shot full of heroin
behind the beat, her gravity
made light by the subjective strains
of celebratory lyric
spiked with homeopathic snake venom.
Poetry's oligarchs are czars
self-interested autocratic fakes
corrupt as the globally hunted Blairs
shielded by suited thugs.
Frendz No.31
the Uncle Bill interview issue, WS
shotgun Burroughs in a Savile Row suit,
a thin alien futures intelligence
a blue light round him chased from substances
like a neutrino burning off
at light speed—he paid John Brady
his Duke Street live-in Dilly rent
£5 a day—Bill on bankable words—
'We must find out what words are and how they
function. They become images when written down,
but images are words repeated in the mind and
not the image of the thing itself.' WB
I never spend a day not gunning poetry
into equivalent fuzzy
reality, the body extended
to its local geography
through words, the acquisitive imagery
I pull from inner space
like wormholing across the galaxy

producing altered physics
clean as a guitar lick or quotient
of chocolate dopamine.
Writing for me involves a family
of weirdos like friendly bacteria
E.coli coded in the gut, I mean
the friends who happen in my poetry
as real-time people who inhabit it
like chromosomes, they're my gene soup,
John, Aaron, Peter, Colin, Toyoko,
Gem, Monika, Wakako,
Jamie, Chikako, Florina, Bill,
Su, all the walk-ins to my lines
orange and fizzy like Redox Vit C
my useable metabolized
in red Silvine note books, and Lisa too
filling my poems with a voice
shaped by the orange Californian sun
so resonant it floats in me
like a violet sunbeam coaxing lyric to
a morning glory's pink and blue
effusive corolla, a shattering
into the light. The thing to do's
mix poetry into the gritty crunch
of randomness, of course I wank
while writing if the need comes up
to explode orgasm somewhere
into the accident. I like to play
'Sister Ray' full on through earphones
to bleed noise into neural stimulus
when hoiking into bravura lyric
because it's my way of accessing blues
viscerally in the London days
messaging my impetus, cab by cab
amber lightning Shaftesbury Avenue
the speed and air pollution in my blood
carbon monoxide (CO) nitrogen dioxide (NO2)
ground level ozone (O2) particulate matter (PM 10)
sulphur dioxide (SO2) hydrocarbons

cocktailed into my in-breath and out-breath
the poem's bits oxygenated
by chemicals inside my word-attack
like a California King snake
uncoiling to a black and white laser
I want that sort of image bite
to feed on me eating Tortilla chips,
the blue, glycaemic index 86,
the blue corn arresting my sense of taste
and working blue into the line
like an Egyptian blue that best upgrades
into the spacy colour
of scattered blue light wavelengths
I call imagination, lift
Into another level like blue bubbles
ticking over carbonated poetry
the blues again—
'It's awful hard to take it, it was such a
bitter pill,
t's awful hard to take it, it was such a
bitter pill,
if the blues don't kill me that man's mean-
ness will'—Ma Rainey—
arrested in a Chicago room
for same-sex sex, legs in the air
like curvilinear black lianas
mauve silk tie knotted at the throat
a sequined gypsy bandana
a dike phrasing vaudeville blues
and couldn't care less, just like me
who couldn't give a fuck for poetry
unless its curve comes off the street
like food at the Stock Pot—Colin's favourite
when dealing drugs, he keeps his stash
in a resewn interior, his fly
a cocaine ecology
for Soho—Cecil Court to Godwins Court
an exogenous periphery
to stashing fingerprinted dirty cash

into resistant energy
the man who's never early for the man
who waits with a habit
to remetabolise—and made to hate
the shape-shifting hustler
who walking the dog's always late.
(Billy, Willy, Wil, Willie, Bill)
the simmering hypnotic London rain
turning me on to subversion,
poets need update every second year
if they're to outlive themselves
as regenerative celebrities
face-up to gin clear thunder rain.
Sonnet 99
'When in the boredom of my wasted days
I turn up photos of old movie stars
most of them dead, the others bitchy gays
and match a poem to them in the bars
I hang out in and fix on just one face,
a hand, a foot, an eye, lips—it's the look
I see compressed in you now in this place
that wins my attention like a pop hook.
When you're in love it seems most poetry
was written to describe the big event
but always falls short, like the way I see
you throwing shapes in our colour moment.
We're most of us stuck in our present time
where poetry by law's a sort of crime.'

The poet as criminal's the one way
to slap convention with a leather glove,
poetry's best pissed out in consonants
in Goodwin's Court, an atomized rainbow
with a gold streaming lion's mane
dispersed to liquid graffiti
as a diagrammatic sign
on London concrete—or is urine vowels
in the black tentacles it leaves.
I'd like to make a poem look
like six Dale Chihuly chandeliers

spaced evenly in a lobby
like frozen blue and purple fireworks.
Today I take the 20 steps
down to the sub-street Phoenix bar
aqua and emerald cove-lights
a signature of white chrysanthemums
like stars concentrated on stems
and Maurice the underground Big Brother
monitoring each new entry
with an instinctual iris scan
the ethics guardian in a scarlet chair
maintaining cool—his flavour of the week
getting another squirt of scotch
and bitching gossip—Maurice knows the lot
like singles riding on the charts
and instantly forgotten—boyz who rent
and those on fringes where the call
is looks and the subtitle arts
their carrot red hair opportune
as optimistic tomato sunshine
checking into Wardour Street.
Thin, ubiquitously lager-sipping
Bill Maurice is the paradigm
of camp attention and so kind
he moves through me like a tasselled
shower curtain of liquid chutzpah
most nights at 6 p.m. like raising sand
into vertical column
sparkly as light broken by a diamond
into scintillating dispersal.
Maurice the bar diva of Cecil Court
is molecularised into my lines
by style and compassionate attitude
and comes up from his mirrored fort
as the consoling friend I need
prepared under Charing Cross Road.
Nobody, even me, reads poetry,
and yet its streamlined minimal payload
seems better designed for big city hits

of distraction than the novel's
linear filler, all that narrative
like empty office space at night,
the lights left on and CCTV
sighting grey shapes like jellyfish
inhabiting the grainy image-bank.
The novel's wrong architecture,
a rectangular brain, a block
of discontinuous intelligence,
the poem's closer typographically
to DNA helices, pasta twirls
of spiky imagery condensed into
a bullet: the novel's too long
300 pages that could be 30
of ramped up corporate incentive
putting a tower in the sky:
the poem fits into a condom foil
as a verbal prophylactic
ready to mind-fuck as port of entry.
Poetry's never had a king
like Elvis, gelled hair dyed black as leather,
biker black and a look that mean
it shook America like a cocktail,
Elvis' stylist Homer 'Gill' Gilleland
oiling his hair obsidian,
his quiff decompressed to collapse
in shattered splintered stands
like black spaghetti, a jet cliffhanger
Memphis Ted rocker pouty cat
spearheading rock—he got the southern blues
accelerated in his veins
like a muscled Mustang GT, the rip
white—knuckle riding USA
like an impacting fault line, Elvis born
in Memphis Egypt a pharaoh
teleported to Memphis Tennessee
as teeny delectation,
skinny, kitsch, rhinestoned clothes bought at Lansky's,
the testosterone phenomenon

slick masculine androgyny
giving a white face to black beat
an urgent amped up instanteity
sexualizing the blues to raw
pelvic torsions, poetry's never had
a pin up or an energy
travelling that way outwards from the hips
as pandemic dissolving
social class like sugar in tea,
a rock/pop/doo wop/blues hybrid
bisexualizing a generation
with shamanic rocker androgyny
that poetry missed out on, genes
and hormones in denial of the beat
burning across the U.S.A.
to London and the skinny Rolling Stones
cooking muddy punk rips of R&B
from Muddy Waters and Delta gurus
like Howlin' Wolf and Chuck Berry,
Elvis who graduated to a black
buffalo pilled-up on a satin bed
bloated with burgers cocktailed every drug
opiates and amphetamine
to sustain the de-idealized myth
of the Kitsch lame Memphis King
whose voice unzipped the 50s like a skirt
slashed open on black panties,
his style the adaption of generic
sexual ambiguity to a cool
hypnotic as strawberry car paint, a finned
Cadillac as paradigmatic
to modern thrust big as a swimming pool
and customized in leopard print,
gizmos blasted across Route 66.
Elvis' last prescription read
like a short pharmaceutical poem
an eight line Nichopolous stanza
packed with excessive whiteout opiates
clustering for E's receptors—

Aug 15'77
Dialudid—50-4mg.tab
"   —20cccc -2mg sol
Quaalude 150—300mg.tab
Dexedrine 100—5mg.tab
Percodan 100 tabs.
Amytal 100—3 gram caps
12 half gram amps
Biphetamine 100 20 mg. spansules

George Nichopolous MD
R x No. 23137 AD30795

It's like a metaphysical poem
this pathway to a chemical exchange
in Elvis brain chemistry, Dexedrine
rhymes with amphetamine,
you get a half-rhyme shared by Dialudid
and Quaalude
and picked up on the edge by Amytal
so that reorganized the prescription
could be configured by John Donne's
tricky stanza intricacy
to an OD remix—Elvis' last
acute drug attack cushioned by Pepsi
before blowing the fuses in his heart
an elephantine post-human
290 pounds, shoe size 11,
shirt size neck 15, motto TCB,
height 6'0"—a cholesterol industry
in mauve pyjamas imploded
into cryogenic Elvisology—
before the leap in quantum geography
back to the Dilly, furry London rain,
peppermint green ads sequenced into blue
and ruby logos, pixelated fonts,
the energetic sell just distraction
increasing nervous edge, the place
an artificial beach, its urban curve

a sexual vocabulary
for desperados—damage on both sides
of the transaction, A-side/
B-side warp—I never came out right
but often made a friend
through money-grimed symbiosis
I mixed with a spoon full of light
in which photons turned into diamonds
and came up shine as poetry
you can't believe. The nearest Ashbery gets
to holding my attention is 'Fragment'
the same-sex intimations coming up
like bumpy nuts in soft nougat
as impact craters in confectionery;
the poem scorched like an omelette's
deliberately ruined accident.
Sometimes I go back to the black railings
to grip my loss, the past I can't retrieve
because we're wiped out
like endemic planetary waste;
Aids unplugged a generation,
the subway steps have lost their dignity
for those with cool bravura attitude
and looks that kill in tubed on skinny jeans.
Bacon on self-revulsion, (he mashed up
the fall shorts from high octane energy)
'How can I take an interest in my work
when I don't like it?' his bovver-boy fist
hassling the paint as laval expression
into randomly imploding fall-out,
a detonated orange smashed on black
a face erupting from assault
and poetry should hurt like that
the neural line emerging hot
from combative chemistry. The rip
again, another sonnet thrashed
into a remix. Sonnet 98:
'Not marble, nor the glitzy trashy graves
of pop stars will outlive this muscled rhyme,

but you'll shine brighter each time a word saves
the bite that makes poetry into crime.
When war crunches a city to meltdown
and looters rock subsiding masonry
you'll still live on as a rumour in town
compact in my resistant poetry
and outlive death like that and enmity
at who you were because you're in my lines
that for some reason win posterity
in a world where only corruption shines.
You're like the summer pop lovers recall
thinking back then to when they had it all.'
Bring Billy back, he probably wouldn't care
like me a fuck for poetry,
but do it like surges of graffiti
to kill time, blow it all apart
the boredom and the autocratic czars
in armour-plated shatterproof
Jaguars—Blair and his psycho entourage
talking torture over rare steaks
drenched in depleted uranium.
I met a man, ah ha, another man
on Sherwood Street one aqua afternoon,
his pill blue eyes and beach blond hair
addressing my aesthetic, thin, fifty,
the biz, he'd managed Bassey's
big spender vocal rocks, the gold
in her expensive showy timbre
solid as 995 purity bullion
emoting at a scarlet apogee
dramatizing loss to a furore
a high ceiling jewel-dripping altitude
that blew holes in this man I met
in a Liberty shirt, a Haxby
city poplin, D, a white check
patterned with pink flowers (detoned floral)
Daks slacks, energetic wallet
protruding—the honest name Sam
or just a Dilly alias

a monosyllabic placebo
on an unimpeachable identity—
I didn't know, you never trust a name
in big city anonymity—
he had a room at Brown's: sobriety
that cost at the English Tea Room
Taittinger, Organic Bohea Lapsang
as a neutral prelude, red cakes
the colour of Californian sunsets,
and edgy consternation about sex
and why I picked up there for poetry
with my sophisticated looks—
'I mean usually they're spotty trade
little rough rhinestones with a hex
and blade'—Sam didn't seem the type
to fish the Dilly underground's
lugubrious black waters for disease,
needles and teeny banditry, its curve
of outlaws like a moody chain
of HIV molecules. And his cock
was like a gherkin, undersized
but explosive in a fluent blow job
that glittered diamanté glue
over a cryogenically preserved sheet
as signatured evidence
of why his cash point clean notes fed my hand
enthused lyrical energies.
He doesn't know he's turned up in these lines,
a day in the life excerpted
from entrepreneurial facilities
and colored like strawberry dessert.
He's in me though, linked to my narrative
like mitochondria, sex stays
as something written into memory
and sold adopts a spiral twist
in chemical pathways and bought retains
a biographical receipt,
a printout recording the time and place
as detailed as the grainy map

on a walnut, the body and the face
retrieved, so too the incongruity
of body shopping. I remember Sam
and all the others met by accident
at Piccadilly in the reversed time
I use to retrack the event,
the hormonal clusters that lead a man
to take on danger in a place
where vulnerability's so acute
it's local dialect, the law
of encounters one of accepted signs
transmitted on a rainy day
below the stairs. To sell you had to look
and buy the collection of parts
that have a punter stand out in the crowd
as recognizably dodgy,
it's always in the no-colour emotions
the give away, the cornered eyes
that never focus centrally,
the sex-shopping paranoid inventory
of local danger studied at a glance,
I know them everywhere, the urban wolf
tracking a scent, the edgy predator
and his predicative prey.
I want to change the subject to patisserie
tarte aux fraises, tarte au citron,
profiteroles au chocolat, millefeuille,
cakes as a sort of poetry,
cupcakes as confectionery metaphor
black bottom cupcake, or a blue
magic cake with fondant artwork
and jam filler—I'm a detail addict
obsessed with minutiae, a fetish spotter
for labels, buttons, barcodes, lists,
words, glitter, glamour, outtakes, rarities,
and any weird subject for poetry
like AHAs, collagen, elastin, free radicals,
humectant, hyaluronic acid
and peptides—if you're a poet

you'll write about the lot, the lingo's good
for subverting poetry into pop.
I'd like to write poetry to Manga
and perform to striptease soundtracks
a sleazy bluesy 'Love For Sale'
sung like it's written on the wall
in lipstick for dystopian burlesque
in a nuclear bunker—words are drag
coating ideas with blue fictions
the blue sky writing, when I'm at an end
I listen to Marc Almond's voice
for torch song compassion—the hurt so deep
I feel it in my own, the hit
a seamless unity, the pain
Oh do it to me baby do
because I'm indigo blue, blue
as the bottom of a broken heart.
I need that contact from the only voice
to the only poet, and today
outside Liberty dark blue hyacinths
(sometimes I think they're lavender
or Evian cap blue or blued-up violet)
point to spring, their bubble-wrap curls
condensed with winter scent, January cold
turning the sky diamond light blue,
a 747's fins frisking through low cloud
like footnotes to amnesia,
the things I remember come back as words
against whiteout blanks, the missing time
that wipes data like a virus
from almost everything we live,
so recall's more like quantum wormholing
into a parallel space-time.
The hyacinth's like a purple pineapple
sheathed in a snake-green Pucci dress
like the one in which Monroe was buried.
Bacon on life/art 'All artists are criminals,
I used to housebreak for adrenalin
now I steal bodies for the studio

not fridge, I used to meet a cannibal
in Brompton cemetery, Jimmy the tooth,
he bought organs stored in a hospital
and picked at them like a gourmet
once with the Krays: he set the table with guns
instead of spoons, a knife and fork,
Ronnie told me about it over tea,
the brothers broke into my studio
and stole my rejects to sell back to me
to break up as botched autopsies
over my knee. Queer London was secret as blood
mapping the arteries, I miss
its cellars, palare, the corridors
East and West choked with sailors,
rent, barebackers, bikers, dockers,
and me crawling on my knees
for mercy.'
                    Bacon's leather coat
was dusted with fine particle pigment
orange and pink raw asthmatic
contaminant. His vitamin B shots
worked to support immune breakdown,
this man in recombinant war
with physiognomy and whacking it
into altered perception, hating age
but converting it into a quotient
of endgame energies—the last attack
that detones black into dark blue,
lipstick red into cerise, but holds up
with orange like a song and green
as reconstitutional. Bacon's life
was everything poetry lacks,
temerity, optimal risk, punky
execration, a jet of piss
writing rainbowed contrail on the wall,
you swallow or interpret it
as a genetic book in an alley—
a schlock metric DNA
fizzy with enzymes. And each time we met

the metric brake, he closer to the end
and I telling him 'Stories of Johnny'
a Marc Almond hit compressed feelings
into 3 mins about smoke and mirrors
and rent reconfiguration—
there's always somebody in life for you
no matter that the bottom line's
so irremediably blue. So blue.
So blue, so blue.
I lived at 39/22 Park Crescent
020758093993
and sometimes phone to hear the absent me
sucked into the city's vortex
of deletables. We move like ETs
across the city, genetic error
programmed in DNA like frozen blood
showing traces of HIV.
I'm nobody, a detonating squirt of words
with a poet's identity.
Billy never wrote to be on the stacks
but valued anonymity.
I'll try again for a time reversal
to relocate his chemistry
in what I do with info in my blood
at South End Green. Sonnet 93.
'Why does my poetry seem dosed by drugs
as though I can't metabolize the new?
Why do I need a gang of Shoreditch thugs
to show me how to beat words black and blue?
Why can't I break the circuit and come out,
my style's so recognizably my own
that every word I write carries the clout
of my ID and everything I've known.
These days I wrote of you like a habit
that goes unmodified, I've lost the zing
and can't get out of words the ruby hit
that gives them update and makes the language sing.
My love for you's consistent like the sun
Shining on whatever we've lost and won.'

A catastrophic red sky over the West End
strawberry over Piccadilly
the Blairs have brokered World War 3
from their gene soup pathologies.
I go see Colin, get some valium
to round my angularity
as lucky blues, buy a black Zen iPod
to fire-up my creative chemistry
by putting noise directly in my brain
and speak of laundering money
as still another form of poetry
that's subversive copy. The rain
comes on as trancy, conciliatory
over downgraded Peter Street
this man in a charcoal chalk stripe Crombie
convicted for two murders
as Kray Brothers extortionist, his voice
deep as a whiskey shot crooner
full of street legend, its amber tone
like tangy J&B, his purple scarf
pulled from the rainbow. Arms up to the sky
he sings 'Day in Day Out'
on red alert, throwing colors with words
there on the pavement, I can hear
his personality mixed like a drink
with raw bluesy a capella,
the grain in his voice the closest I'll get
to ever knowing how his hurt's
released impromptu, exhibitionistically
in phrasing, Colin's direction
gone with the song. He tells me poetry's
best written on washed money
if it's to enter the mainstream. He steals
his supplements from Fresh&Wild,
his bread from Convent Garden—'if you're gay
you shouldn't have to pay
for anything—the hurt should be maintained
by a corrupt society.'
Creativity's my big orange sun

like a molecular juicer
turning my neurons oranger, my line
to addictive upgrade poison.
It's a process that what you lose you win
by recreating it, I've lost
everything over and over, the all
of it still not experienced.
The sky's that orange it's like an orange lolly
solidified into granules,
and what I see is like a glitter ball
suspended over Wardour Street
in atmospheric shattering. I write
a poem on my wrist you'll never know
or miss a purple Pentel tattoo,
I'm street trash and my only rule
is to break every recognizable taboo
in putting shine on poetry.
My fans always treat me like a pop star
their presents colouring my life,
books, shirts, flowers, a splash of glitzy paste
for performance, endless update
of my obsessions, feeding nerves like fish
with pellets that explode as camp.
I'm never offline to inspiration
it comes up in neural revs
waiting for John to walk into the line
with no disconnect, I write fast
into a friend's conversation, full-on
like driving talking on the phone
as bilocated multitasking telepathy.
Poetry don't reach anyone
'cos it's monopolised by sterile greys,
but it's still lively as a strawberry
to catch on the tongue so vivaciously
it's pepper mixed with tart
nostalgic taste-bud abrasions. I read
maybe thirty poems a year
randomly and in bits, some Ashbery,
some Wieners, Berrigan's Sonnets,

just for a sugar fix of imagery,
a phrase that I assimilate
chipped in my neurology. Life's so fast
a poem modifies its speed,
it's a smart event like a blue smartie
discovered in the predictable mix,
red, orange, green, yellow, lavender, brown,
a blue artificial planet
glowing with turquoise luck in my cupped hand
as an instance of poetry
dipped into on the street. Today I themed
my work with Billy Fury's voice
the ultimate tearjerker crooner blue
pixellating teardrop pop,
the Elvis inflexions a Liverpudlian
Mersey scouse meets deep Tennessee
the voice catch just like eating your heart out
with the knowledge you're bound to die
before you live. Billy's phrasing
is full of heart medication and loss
at twenty-one—digoxin in his blood
the foggy docks sunk in his chest
as an insupportable reminder
of green tides that he'd left behind, his voice
carrying the song fractionally sharp
like Frankie Valli, but the signature
so inimitably his own it hurts
like riverboat accents in fog
arced into spotlights on a Vegas stage
in Great Yarmouth—a green, a red
light building colours in his blownback hair
like he's a continuous star
whose song compacts a little space time,
a suspended 2.50
in which to go missing, attached to pain,
'In Thoughts of You' sung indigo
like someone swimming up from the bottom
with news they'd rather stay on down
than reach the top. Billy's phrasing turns blue

on contact with the air, the ache
like the formation of a bruise, the phrase
like catching gem dust in a glass,
the sparkle in dejection raying out
as uncommissioned broken hope
but there as texture, Billy's three minutes
extended to three million
in listening time: dead in January 1983
of cardiac arrest, his hair
dyed beach blonde fanning the pillow—
an end at 43. Billy sucked
into his legacy—a disembodied voice
re-mastered into bits, a sad blue poet
turned to by the disconsolate
as starry pop.
                                The poem heads
back to the street transporting my info
as neural firing: Bacon there
pulled out the catastrophic shattering
of growing older with the speed
of Big Bang in his blood. 'I won't be there
to know I'm dead and if I am
I'll claim it's mistaken identity
and do a time reversal
to the Colony. I'd like to mix a blue
to have poured over my body when dead,
the one I've never got, a bluer blue
than crashing lapis into manganese,
the colour I imagine as my blue
you get sometimes in dark blue eyes—
I saw that blue once in Harrods Food Hall
and followed the man out the shop
into the underground and took his tube
and managed to sit opposite
to keep that blue moment alive and look
at the colour I couldn't mix
obsessively like an eye thief,
got out with him at Leicester Square
and left him go onto the Northern Line

for fear I'd kill to get a blue
I'll never paint. I imagine the headline
Artist kills for the colour blue
he saw as pigment in somebody's eyes.'
I met a man, ah ha, another man
who walked out of the street's grainy footage,
the sunset like tomato juice
choked with carbon emissions in his look,
urban data coded into his genes
another loser ramping up his luck
in excruciating exposure—
the street as raw public domain
for impulsive illegal encounter.
Ben was neurotic anti-HIV
autophobic, so scared of the virus
he did air-sex even air-kissed
hand tooling his eight-incher
on dissociated autopilot,
pathologising the body as AIDS,
a viral supernova of disease
waiting to explode from B-side contact,
Ben thought you got it from panspermia
or even handjobs in a club
or food sprayed with reversed-bacteria
or me just giving him support
with his full on obsessive phobia.
I cared about him more than poetry
that evening, the night coming on
like a blue diamond shot with stars
rayed out across the galaxy,
I really did strange things at the Dilly
keeping in mind. I told myself hold on
it's only temporary,
the way traffic lights change
from red to amber in a flash
programmed to meet the city's thrust.
The years I've left back there are hologrammed
molecularly into me, my own
debate with meeting London in the street

done this way—you can't know the lot
but the best come out of the rain
looking to buy a skinny prototype
of disaffected attitude,
defiant rent like a blind dip
into a chocolate box—I'm purple foil
and you're triangular green.
I've searched so many faces in the crowd,
the film never once on repeat,
the question one of relativity,
the faster I move the more time slows down
like going off in a spaceship
at speed of light and finding on return
I'm younger than when starting out.
I feel that some days, everyone's older
than my reinvented burn
my constantly updated re-entry
to poetry like going to Drury
on New End Row to buy black chocolate
77% active ingredient
the day made real by the endorphin surge
a little up on Garrick St
a brief psychoactive supernova
with a saturated aura
making things better with the London blues
of course I'm bound to die
between two pushy river tides
maximum entropy in the liver
my name written on my disease
if I'm discovered. I'm preoccupied
these days with why the Stones are so skinny
so anorexically guitar-neck thin,
their paradigmatic teeny figures
maintained at 28-30 waist
despite the dinosaur tracks on their skin
the dehydrated leather warp
burnt in by drugs and booze and nicotine
to epidermal mapping, pits
like tyre-treads on a Jeep, a regolith

of rocky hedonistic tours
riffed by excess slashed like fault lines
into their features, but they're still
hungry-waisted emaciated czars
avocados, goji berries, brown rice,
wholemeal pasta, grains, pulses, sushi, fish,
high carbohydrates and no fat,
Jagger's diet, and no-one else but me
will ever theme it as subject
for poetry: a poet/dietician
no fat in his poetry,
no hypogenated phrasing, my waist
like the Stones 28-30,
an enduring size zero consistency.
Today the 'Gimme Shelter' riffs
avian rumble like hanger reverb
still fires up a neural response
like anticipating summer thunder,
prescient, premonitory,
a purple imploding into aural blue
so menacing it's like a quango
accounting for terrorist reprisals
the power-chords reverberating
like a decommissioned aircraft
slamming over towers
in executive storm. It finds me out
as programmed in my cells, a riff
fusing two modern centuries
in a dystopian soundtrack
like a smoking gun. It's the last sound
the world will hear before meltdown
burns with a screaming line of jets
nosecone through towers, a red rip
mushrooming into an explosive plume
of detonating kerosene,
'Gimme Shelter' marauding the earphones
of urban kamikazes—a Stones riff
pulled from the London blues delta,
Chelsea Harbour way. Gimme pop

for brain reward, orange euphoria
as a 3mins auroral supernova
fed through I-pod plugs at death.
                                        Bacon on death—
'Death's an imaginative reality
it's anything you want it to be
a black shape on the edge of time,
a syringe full of black liquid gold
or something so close up, familiar,
it's always been there like the sighting wall
staring us down in the bathroom
from clinically stainless steel fixtures.
For me it's all the suicides
left in the fridge I can't forget
come out at me as cryogenics,
dead meat and sex and Vitamin B shots
as the extended legacy
of things I can't forgive myself like spaghetti
in the wrong sauce with parmesan
instead of grated pepperoni,
George Dyer ordered fish and chips
at L'Escargot—I made the waiter go
and buy them legitimate
on Shaftesbury Avenue—Billy Walker's
and serve them wet, degraded, flat.
Death's created by the living, a fact
we can't negotiate, an end
that's pathological—I couldn't care
but back of everything I do
about death as a package—what's in it,
like a condom packed in a foil
the idea we go on as time travel
a teleported conscious chip
is opposite to everything I paint
the density of flesh, the mass
of purple that I feel as body weight
when painting, when I lift the pigment
it's like shifting a human form
or slapping wet flesh, epidermal grain

that smells of horse. If I'm a shape-shifter
I'm also a docker, the sort I fuck
because I lift with the paint, orange pigment
heavy as carrying a man
up river steps—could you carry Shakespeare
drunk up the stairs at Bermondsey
and throw him rain-soaked into poetry
like I support Dyer in paint
his dead body slung over my shoulder.
I've died so many times like that,
blacked out in the studio—I couldn't care—
drink does that and crawled on the floor
looking for something I knew wasn't there
and instead found a bottle by the door
I'd broken my head on for A&E
to be stitched up like one of my portraits
done aubergine whacked with red impasto
and ultramarine.'
                                        Today my new shirt's
subject of poetry again, Sherry's
a turquoise motif over white,
back collar button, back pleat, button down
and catches me out in between
the lines I write: poetry fills in space
as detail like making a shirt
from Mod pattern, like DNA Groove
Vicenza, whose 3" collar height
gives a cotton fortress build to the neck
released into 5" collar points
arrested into button downs. The trick's
to hang the collar like a skier
suspended on a slope: two white spear points
unleashed on strawberry,
the front fastening buttons secured in twos,
the mother of pearl buttons glossed
like marbled floors, it's the acute detail
engages it as poetry—
DNA Groove making a hot debut
in poetry as brand names, I'm the one

who brokers labels in my work,
full sewn pleat front and back,
pointed back collar; the rain outside today
the colour of the London sky
a gin and tonic river fizz, a grey
like a smoky opal throwing shapes
a grey eye flecked with green and blue
wide open on a foggy sea,
a rain outnumbering my brain neurons.
I've never got this close into
doing writing, all distinctions dissolve
between me and glamorous glue—
palare for sticky come, poetry's
like wanking reality
into explosive metaphor. I keep
a clipping of the mutant alien
Michael Jackson in an L.A. bookstore
for Martian input as I write,
we both have silver blood metabolites
and think in purple imagery
incantatory as Xanadu,
that one-off mantra got from opium paste
as an informative psychoactive.
Michael's surgical face mask kills
random bacteria, his fedora
sits like a black felt UFO on his head,
he carries an umbrella in the shop
to keep from contamination,
people are a species free-radical
he avoids at 50, his red lipstick
a postmodern postfutures signature
most possibly a matte red Mac
mixed with an offbeat pigment for his tone.
He's simply nothing but a star
in every mitochondrial gene
visiting his Beverly Hills doctor
to talk of white pigment toxins
piloting MSRA in his cells
that deconstructs his nasal bridge and grooves

backs of his hands to raw lesions,
the alien bankrupted and blown into
financial disorbit, his star
discredited and smashed apart and shot
into a slow liquidating fall out.
                                        Bacon on pain—
'It's the basement, the backroom where we know
an ontological black gold
that's like a probiotic to the gut
something we need like bouillabaisse
on Thursdays or Beluga caviar,
a spoonful sipped to stimulate
awareness that a sturgeon's ripped open
to colour up a taste. I need
to shatter by breakfast like a psycho
bulleting through re-entry
to sanity from a delirious space,
sex, brutal humiliation
and chronic alcohol, the London night
drenching me with toxicity
and pain carried inside me like carbon
converted to a black diamond
by morning—mornings at Reece Mews—the light
still the colour of inner space
that's so variously pixellated
there's no pigment match, no no-colour match
but somehow over Fortnum's marmalade
and a first drink I get a feel
to mix it somewhere between grey and pink
or red and silver or I've tried
neutral charcoals sexed up by green
to get an industrial feel
to inner real. And once I sliced my knee
to get the lesion into tone
and knew a lemon-squeezer surge of pain
scorch me with electricity
trying to lift Dyer's taut pectorals
onto the canvas, shape-shifting
physique into virtual and paint's

the nearest to accessing DNA
I know because I'm the contact
who works it to the ministry
of imagination under Vauxhall
or any place where sex does pain
like the fisted whack in my art.
You can't access weird if you're straight,
you lack the codifying gene, the kink
that criminalises what you see
into same-sex perception, straights don't do
detail or up colour tempo
like jumping up and down on strawberries
to bleed cerise to violent red.'
I tell you I've watched my contemporaries
in poetry liquidate anyone
like me who won't be cashed by oligarchs
into a policed conformity,
I'd rather be a cult, a concealed dance
taken up on a Soho floor
in a weird configurative way,
a scratchy beat, a beaten trick
matching a red shoe with a blue
and thought of on a rainy day
as doing ballistics with imagery
in ways that look towards the new
like a runway projected at the sky
for queuing planes. I couldn't care
a fuck for careerists in anything,
just adventurists sold on risk
who'd do it anyway without reward
for friends like buying a bottle
that doesn't last, but adds an edge to edge
in listening to new sounds, or sharing pain
over a common grief or bill
arrived on red alert. I used to write
lying on John Robinson's painted floor
as though poetry belonged there
right down in a glossy white textured grain
at Natal Road, a wine bottle

in grabbing reach, Frank O'Hara's poems
saturated in sunlight squeezed
like lemon juice through the Venetian blinds
there for support, or Barry Macsweeney's
image-rich Odes, the language like nougat
cratered with almonds and cherries
and so outrageously anti-mainstream
I'd read his mimeo'd pamphlets
like locking with a drug. I learnt down there
the bottom's just the op reversed
only it's steadier. John's room spilled mags
and books and Tequila bottles
and yoghurt packs, strawberry, blueberry,
French vanilla and poetry
like no one else, all the Americans
we read for sunny vitamins
and modern enzymes, like Larry Fagin,
Ted Berrigan, Ed Dorn, Kenward Elmsie,
Steve Jonas, Robert Duncan, implant genes
the colour of hope resistantly blocked
by British poetry like a protease inhibitor
increasing CD4 cell counts
to combat copy. The poetry police
moulded to power like concrete,
the quango—Paterson, Armitage,
Motion, O'Brien, Robertson
fucking each other with prizes
killing off changes to maintain
a concentrated mediocrity.
You don't go troubleshooting on their patch
unless you're me, and the payback's
annihilation, crunching a small art
into the size of a power breakfast plate.
The free go to the underworld
where poetry belongs with criminals
and damage and the bits blown out
of breakdowns. That's my natural zone
the gravitation to losers who shine
like rubies in the dark and stay down there

without concession to their state
and never come up right. If I've lost out
I've used poetry like a drug
in a lab test to explore every cell
connecting with its chemistry
the way sharks see in colour in mid-sea
and still I have to make a way
in living from an art that doesn't pay
my rent—it's John Wieners' story
re-lived as mine, the same
disparagement for being different
by civil servant polymer
mentality: there's a big scarlet sun
facing down over Marble Arch
back of my hand like a red traffic light
writing this inside Selfridges,
the shop windows lit like a Campari
swirled round for the fizz of soda
into a sensual Mimi Holiday pink
and back on the street it's fine particles
eat even regenerative face creams—
lipopeptides working to firm
the skin with sodium hyaluronate
simply a Boots skincare restorative
to help keep age reductionist.
Its formula's like an anthology
of dermal poetry, ingredients
a sexy postmodern cocktail
rejuvenating as probiotics.
I look for lists as future poetry,
read-out mantras on jams and processed food,
pesto sauce and tahini
instructive as Ted Berrigan's sonnets
or hair spray; the sky's coloured like money
today, dollars, pounds, rupees, yen, Euros,
city lights like currency
you pay to occupy its space
checking in from the galaxy
and choose a colour that's available

for appropriation inwardly
as molecules like champagne fizz,
the slabs I write under like gold
cemented over, glass cladding, a cube
as corporate monolith in the sky
up there like architecture snorting coke
to maintain a skyline hegemony
with troubleshooter bankers in Paul Smith
using handgun tactics on growth
to slap opponents. And I couldn't care
providing I spike-up a line
vitaminised with the city's enzymes
like gold dust floating on bacteria
in my hyperactive nanosecond
that's life. You haven't heard the least of it
the men I've met, the black paint on my hands
burnt from the Dilly railings
as mark of my profession, love for sale
at a price—no one got to me
for keeps or ever got into my head
to see the poem living free
of dirty money, like an orange sun
risen in me, autonomous,
untouchable, the sex so secondary
the punter always got locked out
into the thing he couldn't buy
the illusion of me
as resilient compliant meet.
But still I'd rather the worst there
than any fake airhead in poetry,
money as issue, cash for flesh
like killing elephants for ivory
and leaving every sinew rot
under the street on Shaftesbury Avenue.
I'd go home so strung out I saw
hallucinated faces in the lights,
red, blue and green phenomena
facing me down in Soho in a grid
I know by every mews and yard

and met Derek Jarman one night pissing
in D'Arblay Mews, I too in need
of slashing hot stream in that dark alley
a single flow wattage red light
burning outside a model's door
our urinous calligraphy
a meeting point, his HIV advanced
to an emaciated atrophy
a scorched retroviral kamikaze
copy of self-destructing cells,
his skin so translucent his personality
was at the surface, diamond-bright
neural impulses firing brilliantly
as starlight in his energies,
leather and denim moulded to his cold
fever, and shaking in that yard
like plane turbulence, Derek shook
like an epileptic pissing
into a seizure, toxic sweat
and sarcoma and AZT
and residual chronic pneumonia
both of us urgent in our rip
against a wall he saw as neighbourhood
a Soho sited in his brain
and hardwired to his sexuality
like William Blake on Marshall Street
hallucinating London like a drug a psychoactive capital
ingested for neurofeedback, his mind
manufacturing LSD,
and Derek and I under a red light
attracted simultaneously
by bladder frequency to D'Arblay Mews
creatin and toxicity
atomized as impacting signatures,
a hissy soundtrack to our talk—
I wanted him to film my Isidore
my whacky novel about Lautréamont
he loved, a subversive recreation
of gay youth dead at 22

anonymously in a hotel room
after completing *Maldoror*
the last corrections done in red not blue
as self-harm or a killer's mix
of hemoglobins stuck like glue:
a dust cloud rising over *Maldoror*
like radioactive fallout, off message
images exploding like a heist
liberating diamonds into a sack.
The two of us that furry Soho night
randomising a piss vocabulary
in a still undeveloped yard
Maria's red light glowering on alert
to rubbered need and Derek's back
curved as the toxoplasmosis took hold,
but still resistant, defiant
to somehow keep sighting creative gold
in plague and depredating loss
and viral meltdown in St Anne's parish
a skinny carrier avoided by
taxi drivers, downgraded into sweat
and undercover outlawry,
a man hunted because his viral load
signalled his illness, HIV
leaked on his skin like a purple tattoo
our meeting inside D'Arblay Mews
an opportunistic one-off click
on felicitous synchronicity,
ten minutes spent injecting verbal light
into each other's chemistries
like condensing a lifetime into bits
integrated spontaneously
because support was there as building blocks
a creative likeness that fits
ten years in ten minutes, he gone his way
to a studio at Phoenix House
and I to Regents Park with Derek's voice
like a soundtrack inside my head,
its emotional timbre glowing in me

like cooking a drug on a spoon
to an orange-red euphoric aura
knowing I'd never lose its tone
in moments of inspired need, its lift
like a scarlet anemone
opening into light, despite pain
written into the undertone
like enthusiastic rain dying out
at 7 a.m. over smoky tea
and Frank Cooper's Vintage Coarse Cut Oxford
Marmalade, Derek's favourite too
that he can't taste in death. Later we met
on Brewer Street, his eyes up to the sky
for colour, he could hardly see
and choked on 40 pills a day
like overdosing on toxic smarties
and told me he'd miss sex the most
when dead, the frequency that he'd fine-tuned
by breaking into the body
like a house thief. He had three months to live
as imploded reality
fifty years decompression like a plane
blowing out in the Heathrow corridor
in smoky cloud. Maison Berteaux for tea
then back to intubation, drips
and whatever gritty pleasure survived
in consciousness, that neural jellyfish
rayed out across the dark blue universe
in tracking signals. Today all the way
from Vauxhall Bridge to Waterloo
the tide graduating from blue to green
under the arches, I picked thoughts
out of glittered current with a sky
like a floating aquarium
going over one way to the South Bank
and loopily on to Temple
with clouds like bullet-nosed marauding fish
starting to pile up round the sun,
and there's still greenblack glitter on my eyes

from last night's reading at First Out,
a moody eye shadow called Nightclubbing
a compressed galaxy worked in
as sparkle, reading as the Ginger Light
we packed the place to overspill
under the street, the reverb echoey,
the microphone my focal point
for impacting projection, our set list
filmic, urban with Gerry's beats
sounding edgy as postmodern Berlin,
mixed down so I work on its back,
the cove lights dimmed, my projected élan
like neural helium—we're pop
with poetry, the mirror at my back
an oval, like an astronaut's window
building a space behind that's lit
by table lights, faces and red quasars
and me emoting at the mike
taking the rev up a notch, doing it
like subterranean blues under St Giles,
our set-list bouncing in with 'Nifty Jim'
a tricky shuffling 'Piccadilly Bongo'
the sexy desperation in the mix
winning the place, turquoise sequins
launchpadded like a UFO shower
into a gestural choreography
that don't come easy and won't come again
after we're gone, our little cult
sustained by CDs, video, on-off
residual memories, the shock
of our cellar attack, Gerry McNee
and Jeremy, quirky duo
remaking and remixing poetry,
dance grooves and spoken word and pain
like pins popped in a voodoo doll
and all the red roses given
like hexed romance get stardom in my flat
like lippy diva pouts, that red
they're like strawberry jam, sensual rubies

brimming with entropic volume
to spill all over the floor as an end
like I'll be found there one day dead
from strategically achieved OD
with a banana and benzos
and a bottle of sunlight-blond champagne
and wearing Martyn's customised
purple velvet shirt, blackcurrant stitching
made up by John Pearse for his death
from viral kamikaze Aids, passed on
to me as fetishistic legacy
by his sister with a green poison ring
as components of my death kit
if I assert control and go out last
listening to Marc Almond sing
'St Judy' as diva spectacular
the ultimate purple panacea
to dying outside the system, the voice
the last sustained contact in the blood's churn
towards extinction, Marc's phrasing
addressing pain like pitting a cherry—
'and if I die before I wake up
I pray the Lord don't smudge my makeup'
the last words that I'll ever hear
as aphoristic elegy.
You know I worked the Dilly and the pain's
unshareable except with the punter
because we're linked in creating a pact
of hurting each other in ways
that are the same, like the plum needs the stone
to ripen, and Marc's part of that,
his tone resistant in conceding loss,
I mean so many men cried in my arms
for what they are and couldn't change
same sex attraction, a piloting gene
that eliminates opposites like blue
mixing with green without graduating
to yellow, there's no tertiary involved
just same, the green stone in a ring
I love for being just that tone

a moody jade with a green sea
extending away like a galaxy
and deep as Africa and the gay gene
coded into a sensitivity
that's uncorrupted green containing blue
come up as lapis lazuli.
Mostly local, the Regent Palace Hotel,
I'm paid to listen and hold someone's hand
a stranger like an alien
selecting me for looks—I understand—
a suit called Alfie (43?),
accountant understudied charcoal suit,
compressed voice toneless as money
the hurt he carried a disaster site
impacted in him like a plane
nosed through a bank, he'd been caught cottaging
in a Piccadilly car park
with Miss Singapore a.k.a. Paul Murphy
and charged with public indecency
faced unmitigating holistic ruin,
a partnership, a refrigerated marriage
chilly as vodka frozen for shot,
routinals hardwired to his nerves
as all he knew and me paid £50
for listening to his terminally resigned
abdication of life, he'd planned it all,
the pills, his wife's weekend away,
the insurance—I couldn't turn it round
a man whose one tropical splash
was Dilly rent—the colour he could buy
on the railings turning his grey
into a red and pink tropical sky
brushstroked by revved adrenalin,
his aberrational orgasmic high
always bought, he'd been going there
twenty years as a fugitive punter
been warned twice for soliciting,
got off, been robbed, rolled, but kept coming back
as an addiction to the place,
the Sam Sung, Sanyo and Burger King ads

doing their scarlet LED displays
like turning tricks. I listened to him fade
into irremediable despair
before he cried on the pillow, broken
by emotional shattering,
the whiskey floating off his breath like steam
vaporized from a lake, its heavy pull
sucking into oblivion the way
I knew he'd be dragged down by pills
into a place that's vacuum sealed
and only split open by autopsy
as pathological data, his hurt
exempt from all analysis,
so too emotional pain, degradation
and personal loss gone swimming deep
inside his arteries. I never saw
hope go out quite so terminally
and couldn't do the least thing to reserve
the mad accelerated rip
at which it travelled through his chemistry.
I didn't know his name or ask
knowing he'd lie, and his obituary
elude me as a cold sanitized fact.
I went back outside to the light's
saturated photons at Leicester Square
and sat and didn't move an hour and wrote
a poem submerged in a red notebook
I've lost in time as disinformation
like NASA data, lost the hook
that made it pop and spent his fifty pounds
buying collectable first editions,
the books that build fortress security
inside my flat—Black Mountain stuff
Fulcrum, Cape Goliard, Trigram,
no British poetry, just US guns
blazing with climbout imagery
using America as the format
on which to write—the Brits lack energy
and need a spike of LSD
to get into the shock-waved imagery

that's my natural way of seeing,
a shape-shifting transformative wacky
detonation of energy
that projects at the speed of light—
186,000 miles per second a trick
of bending language with the light
into the brain's grey density
so it shows like 3D video
the Brits don't get it, they're so slow
they're left in the departures lounge
with excess baggage. I got free
by reading America in my veins
as vitamins—Ashbery blew me away
into a blue stratospheric tangent
and Wieners took me to the microphone
as performer, and I'm still there today
Britain's only glamour poet, full on
throwing lyric shapes on the air
configuratively, Oh no it's me
doing a diva on the saddest art
the microcosmic cell that's poetry
killed off by institutional greys
flat as the bath a suicide's turned red
from slashing a network of veins.
I don't expect sympathy for my art
but award purple rainbows to
the ones who took it all—there's Jack Spicer
gone into meltdown on the beach
more whiskey in his veins than blood,
his detonative metaphors
making a rip like a Ferrari tyre
scorched to impacting blowout like a strip
of snake. Robert Duncan on the same coast
aqua CA with lapis lazuli
Pacific pull and foggy bays sun kissed
orange, the metric in the breath
reorganized as lines gravitating
to personal geography, my diaphragm
becomes the centre of the sun
for redirecting metabolized oxygen

into a stream of fired-up imagery
like a NASA shuttle compressed
into component metaphor, the poem
rehabilitating alien intelligence
into its reward system. They've died out
like a rainbow contrail
vaporized like coolant over the sea,
their poems left like prostitutes
in unopened anthologies, red lights
signalling to turn a trick
and ageing, downgraded with no upgrade
like a decommissioned Boeing
oxidized in a hangar. If I knew
the way back to refresh Ed Dorn,
Robert Creeley or Olson's shipbuilding
in a topographical line
I'd go that way, rediscover again
the neural bullet I received
reading their Fulcrum books in summer rain
under a shelter at La Colette
a thunder sky like a polished oyster shell
rumbling over a dark blue sea
my Pinot Grigio bottle half sunk
I couldn't give a fuck for poetry
only its terrorists, not copyists,
Black Mountain then, a black diamond
set in my heart—a mythical black cone
with a guru on it like a cherry
on a rum baba. I never got them right
my imitations—went to J.H. Prynne
for neuroscientific lingual density,
no writing about things, just what makes noise
in brain chatter—I wrote complexity
like quantum physics in the thrust
I gave to poetry, my line a fist
of raw unpolished stones, a jeweller's bag
of Antwerp rocks, a green, a blue diamond,
stormy emeralds, a moody ruby,
a lapidary galaxy of exploding metaphors
compressed like a neural cyclone

into accelerated rip, that's scotch
and valium and Bowie in the mix—
Black Russian Outtakes from the Airman's Club
poems as skewed as altered states
I wrote by the docks, back to a warehouse,
dressed in a purple velvet coat

my energy sustainable all day
like being plugged into the source,
men gave me money just for being me
a poet up against it all,
nerves shot down, a clinical psychiatrist
blocking me on valium,
the little blues I mitted to dissolve
indomitably dystopian reality,
eliminate conditioning by pills
notching up space-times in my chemistry
away from it all—the gravitational well
pulling me down into a black hole
I got above through Bert and Nifty Jim
subverters of my youth who set me free
by crime, shoplifting, queer affrontery
and going underground—the niche
I occupy—the dance groove in my blood
that takes me to the river, a Thames pool
obsidian as a submerged city
floating with raspberry-coloured clouds
and all the trashy ephemera we stole
to hit back at the chains, the quotient
of nothing needed, glitter in the hand
vaporizing in the moment
like a rhinestone contrail of cooling sweat,
disappointment, burnt out adrenalin,
and me sitting there on the sand
counting it out, the paperbacks and paste
and red-framed sunglasses lifted from Boots
all of it deglamourised
in a sparkling consumer pyramid
a heap of disconnected things
Jim kept on reassembling for the thrill

he couldn't recreate in anything
in his post-kleptomaniacal glow,
the flattening of stimulus, the sea
out there as menthol green mixed with peacock
a low-tide twitchy meniscus
pushing its eye in like a psychopath
a bluegreen disk extending round the world
but local to our beach, its blue thunder
so far out in the afternoon
we heard its ambient roar sitting there
demoralized, computing gain
against the loss of coming down big time
into the ordinary day
as nobody, just misfits on a beach
staring in shades at a green horizon
as though we'd sight the future there
like heavy industry built on the moon.
I knew sorting through lighters, shades and rings
that these were bits of poetry
to be integrated into my mix,
component bits of theft reorganized
into a sort of blues, the way sadness
is the baseline to everything
a common emotional oxygen
a sadness like black matter filling space.
I got the blues even happy
and get the blues most every day
and write out of its broken atmosphere
like it's the top not the bottom
I'm coming from, the poem taking stairs
out of the underground to the Dilly—
I met a man, aha, another man
downstairs on the inner circle,
the rammed concourse with DNA traces
of half the world, the up and down
vertiginous shuttle to the platforms,
quizzical faces emerging,
the introspective tensed into descent,
I met Greg in his chalkstripe suit,
a Tommy Nutter I knew by the cut

the little details made as eye candy
like me standing there with my pop star look
patterned button-down, vinyl tie,
four button blazer, the red silk lining
like a poppy split by the wind,
black skinny jeans: Greg dipped his voice
to ask if I was selling sex
and if so I was his selected choice
and it was his place at Tavistock Square
by taxi and a hundred quid
to blow, while he smoked a cigar
dissociatively—the things you do
to fine-tune creative chemistry,
Greg in his Creed or Miller-Harris scent
terrified of plain clothes on the concourse
sold on the desperation of his act—
it's always the first time, the lie
predictable as a duplicitous cover
for compulsion, I never met a man
who didn't tell me it was the first time
he'd paid for it, like spontaneity
had vacuumed habitual restraint
because he couldn't pass me by
knowing we'd never meet again, the rain
outside demanding that we dash
into a black cab on the Haymarket
like Bond into his DBD,
boys in the rain waiting their edgy turn
on the diamond drizzled plaza—
'Pardon me sir, I'm just a damaged poet
with my defences broken down
I'm somebody but you don't know it
baby am I broken down'—
and Bacon squaring up to suicide
like a polyurethane sprayed black armoured truck—
'it's got its colours, black and grey and red
a black depression that weighs like a fridge
you open out to equally black space
like most the universe is black,
dark matter packed between the stars—the lights

of stars so few, they're like a car's headlights
dipped on a loopy bend, there's no way out
of black, it's where we gravitate,
each gene directed towards irreparable error,
the blackness though, my cells convert
it into industry, I've seen a face
upriver of India Wharf, a black,
I've never painted black incidentally
that's like primitive density
worked into jeans and a broad leather belt
a black figure who gives muscle
to pathology, I could fuck him back
of the container yard, my grip
on his black body like peeling the skin
on a banana, black not grey
that neutral intermediary, the light
informing my Kensington day
that's London gray not grey, a city tone
you get in suits that lack silver
and seem like lived-in grey without the lift
of aluminium or mercury:
grey's not liftable in paint and max vo 1
still lacks a personality
that sparkles, grey opals have blue and green
scintillation like a marble floor
molecularised on LSD
into a hallucinated jewel
a 3D prismatic parabola—
I had the thing happen in Mayfair
1968, someone spiked my drink
and I went psychoactive, saw the chandelier
as a UFO I got inside, walked through
a crystal's polyhedral face
into the cabin and couldn't get out
and there were aliens, the common greys
inside, and I could see into their brains
starbursts of neuronal activity,
each brain cell lightning up with its thought shape
so interactive I could see
the sequencing, they gagged me with grey tape

like resistant abductee,
my altered state experiences with grey,
even the caviar seemed jewels,
emerald, blue, ruby micro-spheroids
coalescing into galaxies
on a spoon I lifted with the quasars,
pulsars, neutrinos in the lift,
a mega-impacting mineral burst
resisting taste, an oily supernova,
the party graduating into sex
and flamboyant rock frisson—
it lasted hours that psychotropic spike
and made me negative on grey
as a cake-filler mood-mix, a downer—
sleeping pills should be coated grey
not white or blue, there's so many grey fish,
tuna, mullet, cod and bass
and suicide's an option like a fish
it sights you like a bullet in the brain
  'EXIT'
                    Bacon on suicide at the White Bear.
At Camden Market I can feel the heat,
the jostle of recreational thrust
the spill accelerating from the tube
into a wedge all along the High Street,
indigo clouds stacked over the canal
that's spinach green, a peacock blue
sky arena opening over Parkway:
most Sundays I get snuck into
its gravitational pull, its orbital
impacting whack of energies
and go for retro on the stables side
designer jackets, shirts and ties
that keep me dandified—I mean the look
persists as a recurrent gene,
the ones who like myself put on a face
you don't forget, like a ruby
pulled off the street, a jacket fit, a shirt
moony with polka dots or striped
like three-coloured rain, vertical monsoon

rain, it's linings that fascinate
a scarlet, orange, cerise, gold, paisley—
the jacket's personality
is sewn inside—the brain lining
repeated under pocket flaps
as dominant detail. I've seventy
as image resources, each day
I pull a different jacket persona
as workout for my poetry
and fuck societies who use that name
to kill imagination, you'll find me
writing a signature into the street
as the last focal exhibit
challenging the merger of Armitage
and Motion as the brain—dead greys
proponents of reportage polymer
without an image to fizz up
like bubbles in Veuve Clicquot,
their downgrade so inestimably flat.
There's got to be a last stand in Ham Yard,
my photo shoot the last of Mod
outside the submerged Scene Club's blackened walls
in grainy pixellated Soho light
the colour of Boeing aircraft paint
with Gregory Hesse, he got me
like no other but Mick Jagger
in brooched black blazer, red polka dot tie,
slouched beret on a day with clouds
like blown apart grey chrysanthemums
building conically over Windmill Street
a drizzled diamond light leaking
into the shattered site, I do these things
to spectacularise poetry
like shooting glamour out of a syringe
into a dead artery
and Greg's there digitalizing the feed
we give it, I read round myself
like a circling snake projectively
using the mike as target, who am I
doing this with such shattering intensity

I hold up in optimal delivery
as someone broken by it all,
but resistant to every new put down
as intransigent solvency,
it's my life totally as Bassey sings
so flagrantly individual
her voice seems full of pink and red sequins
arcing in coloratura,
the tone so incontestably sexy
the phrase gets given curves, like Shirley's slink
inside a seamless dress, her tone
so orgasmically ballistic it builds
in graduations to a peak
of naked individuality
molecularised into a voice.
            Bacon on celebrity—
'I always had it even on the street
being on the game makes you a star,
a self-invented fiction: if you're rent
your purple, orange, red and green
and never neutral: it's you owns the bar
and its mirrorball personality,
like wearing a city inside a ring,
London in a fog grey opal,
Berlin in a cold, sharp aquamarine,
Paris an emerald, New York diamond,
everything's nothing, nothing's everything,
money's expended energy
as soon as it's dirt in the hand, we spend
to liberate the need to keep
bad serial impulses, all prostitutes
spend what they earn to wipe the fingerprints
clean off the paper, tainted cash
rehabilitated to the economy
like black sugar, you throw it in the air
like hologrammed confetti
and you're free to work another punter
like a low-grade financier
sighting a level that's below the belt
erogeny and its underworld zones

like a purple testicular tattoo.
Rent's like a flawed coloured diamond,
a fissured navy blue sleeper that shines
for gratification, each warp
integrated into the character
as part of the lugubrious
projection, and I had my share of fines
working the Dilly to buy paint
exploded into unworkable waste
a zero endgaming ensemble
I couldn't sell, like I'd liquidated
my talent without being known
as anything but rent and housebreaker
to anyone in a city
rammed with twelve million. I gave up then
and re-started as someone new
I didn't understand in potential
and how it came up right was luck,
obdurate persistence, just doing it
blind drunk, inspired like London rain
in all its upbeat shattering sparkle
investing everything with hope
by brilliant indifference, one day
the night rain settled with my work
and got into my mood, I could have fucked,
but worked instead and got a face
like skinned chicken dragged about on the floor
and fisted it, got a raw mauve
more cobalt inclined than indigo,
a purple/violet mashed with reds
like autopsy or beetroot, I got space
into the pigment and a hot
pulse in the rainy glow behind it all
and knew I'd found my individual gene
inside the city in high-end Mayfair,
I'd got a room there for illegal things—
gambling, selling sex, extortion,
rumbling the system and I'd got the look
by dragging paint and roughing it
into malleable plasma, pulp texture

I face-lifted with towels abrasively
and as a compensatory thing cramming
on chocolate gateau for sugar
as sticky correlative to my kicks
and somehow the opposite house
rained on by a thundery black grape sky
was part of it, a petunia box
like red and white stripy shirts mashed by rain
but in the moment ledged into
my consciousness, the way imagining
an object puts it in weak gravity,
so you can fit a building in your head
weightlessly, anything you want
to shape-shift individually: that day
I worked paint manually into a riff
I'd come back to as composite,
something to call my own, a concrete thrill,
a dimension broken into, a neutrally fine-tuned access to paint
and what's inside it, like our cells
signature with helical DNA
I'd fingerprinted into character
so unstoppably now I'd got it right
I crammed more cake and physically
fucked with my painting, morphed it into meat
like getting hold a wet docker
around the waist and bending him behind
into a masculine figure, all waist
and entry like a gun chamber; the paint
bumped up in lesions, never flat,
but pitted like makeup, this mashed-in face
was every lover that I'd known
and never reached, because they'd never stayed,
and now I'd fixed the face in paint
as a referential icon it burst
open inside me like a peach
rolled on my apprehensive tongue
as sunkissed measure of a taste
that doesn't classify. I got so high
I trashed the flat, smacked everything
except the mirror I checked in to face

myself as referential map
for an autopsy—I had a blue tie
I'd stolen from Harrods looped round
my shirtless neck, a dark blue silk Jacques Fath
I stained with pink and scarlet paint
and kept on working in an oily sweat
that launched me in the air
feet-first like a bovver-boy's kick
on a Launchpad trajectory
to overtake myself, I'd got it right
as a martini cocktail with the gin
proportionate to pigment and my height
and weight integral to the energy
I metabolized in whacking a face
to disintegration, a scoop
of forensics I managed in a form
that tore through me instinctually
as brutal plasma—I got so far in
I started seeing parallel
like quantum, atoms doing simultaneous copy
in two places—I hit pathways
that exploded with a brushed fingerprint
like sensitive information,
that blew on contact, detonative stuff
I try to energize each day
as variants of one mashed prototype
full of drizzled Kensington light,
I throw most things away or paint over
the partial try-out, it's like surgery,
skin grafts with impasto pigment, alone,
that's why I drink, the solitude's
so saturating, dense as a sorbet
solidified inside to granulated ice—
I've had it up to here and there and there and there
like cryogenics at Alcor,
I'm that locked into the finality
of being me, I've no way out
except through detonating paint, each hit
a facial rip, an excoriation,
a sort of minestrone avalanche

of plasma—and you know I wasn't there
sometimes, I had this Francis clone,
a copy who beamed holograms
into the pulped shattering I called mine.
Today the gin-clear rain's on my own,
listening to the Talking Heads, bubbling hours
at home, like fizzing tonic—
'Psychokiller' and 'Take Me To The River',
a sublingual vocabulary
of associations floored in my genes
like high-rise compact memories,
the songs reminding me of platinum blondes,
dark roots showing, I'll never get
the test hooks out my mind, there's a way words
can only really mean sound,
pop as the sunnier upgrade of poetry,
my size zero status threatened
by extinction—poetry's like the Fleet,
a cold black underground river
infected by Shakespeare's bleeding knee,
dipped in the river Shoreditch
as strawberry haemoglobins dragging by
into a bacterial sewer
networked all over the city, I find
I don't know the right docks or pier
where an opportune reader sits alone
injecting drugs—it's the big H
links psychoactively to what I write
and leave behind like an exploded flat
gutted by housebreakers, my imagery
crunched over by bovver-boys boots
like spiking pingpong balls with stilettos,
the irreversible murder of the word
because it's left defenceless, obsolete
as random space junk noising out of sync
with re-entry—I'll never get it right
except in Japanese bikini statistics—
Height 1.60cm
Weight 44k
Topbust 81cm

Underbust 69cm
C Cup
Waist 61cm
Hip 8.5cm
better than my poem's curve into
universal intelligence, a look
that's cyber-manga-alien aesthetic
and what I'm writing into now
imagining, before Toyoko's eyes
fetch me into the reality
of Japanese, a white skin like a beach
terminating in lazy sea,
a sensual erotic I go into
like magnolias, slippery purple satin
interiors, like sex with Toyoko
a meeting of East/West, a point
dissolved into orgasmic poetry,
thunder breaking over tower blocks
silvering the 21st century
with pixellating showers, a riffy rain
coming on like a stripper, liquid twist
throwing a figure over white highrise
giving shape to the modern light,
its data coded in intelligence
radiated out from the stars.
At Canela in Soho's Newburgh Street
Ben talks of my John Stephen film
the screenplay that I'm writing given beat
and metabolic bravura
by his incentive: a showery Wednesday
we sit with mint leaves in a glass
like aquatic bonsai, a spearmint green
so gastro-incisive the taste's
like relocating a sharp memory
in a popped neural galaxy.
Newburgh Street's seminal to our project,
the starting point for the male look—
Bill Green's Vince frontage, 1953,
a beefcake physique photographer
selling white polo necks and pre-shrunk jeans

and minimal bikini briefs
in candy colours, denim button-downs,
and lipstick pink and red gingham,
a maverick supernova scoping
the red light barrio with firsts,
ace Italian-style copies cut for gays
and blacks with loud colour panache,
the dandified searching out Bill Green's niche
in pixellated Soho rain
for rogue gene gender purchases, a shirt
the colour of a cassis tart
inflected with pistachio, a hat
raked louchely over an eyebrow
as a mean attitude marker, a tilt
under a streetlamp like a dude
in high-heeled boots—they always point one way
towards a bike or cellar bar—
'baby blue you're always a star'
they look straight pretending gay,
arched eyebrows, you can kill a girl that way
and send her back to Leytonstone
alone, sharing a bathroom with a friend
and skincare brands to compensate
for meanness done, of course the street filters
random DNA variants
into the day, and we're at Canela,
the carrot cake a red-orange
like nasturtium, and they should place the flower
as inclusive to taste, a red
like shocking henna, and we stay inside,
projecting John Stephen again
as King of the quarter, his silver Rolls
used as special effects for shoots,
the car a slick aerospace-silver cool,
reconverted now, touch-screened into getaway
like a spray-painted grey UFO. We talk
and time blips through my arteries
like Formula One juice, a burn out I note
in cellular damage, free radicals,
the good and bad. We walk the quarter slow

expecting a quantum pathway
to open out, so 1966
is relocated, shop by shop
as a Mod ripple, suspended displays
of strawberry pink, peacock and grey
denim button downs, gingham creations,
sleek mohair hipsters, blue suede ties,
double-breasted velvet jackets, sensual
as plum coloured spilled peonies,
or black as car paint on a Jaguar,
the ties a silk-tasselled rainbow,
and John Stephen infiltrating his shops
all ears to hear the scooter kids requests
to kill the street with attitude.
He got to be designer king,
the one who got the look so totally
a shirt was like a reported sighting,
that individual in lyric detail
it shone as an original,
a one-off cut from a Soho remnant
you'd never see again, a gold and blue
pattern on a black basis, a mint-green
you'd never recreate, a blue the blue
of pill coating, and we're alone with that
imagined clothes contagion, infectious
Mod pandemic ripping through the alley,
and we're out in a rapping shower
flipping like tiny frogs over the street
each flashy teardrop-shaped raindrop
capping the skin with a tingling alert
to a tonic toxicity—
the taste of London now, strawberry flavoured,
chemical peppermint, carbon
colouring—I'm one in a million
separate by pushing poetry
like a hard drug metabolized on site—
I must be only one in a million
the line Bowie's about Bowie—
the Thin White Duke the Thin White Poet
slung over Dilly railings—'Mister you

won't touch me for a grand, not two,
like Francis Bacon counted out for me
in Denman Street, 'Mister I'm trash
but cash in me converts in poetry
automatically like breathing
I'll show you altered states when I write
a poem like a tattoo on your knee
as punk artistry. Some days I can do
three/four poems as metabolic juice
to doing other conversions, the man
and I, a tenuous balance
like a poppy's full-blown saucer
trembling on a parabola
for just an afternoon, 'Pardon me sir,
it was furthest from my mind,
you're just a thug pretending to be kind,'
the man and I, like fitting words to chords
as chromatic arpeggios,
'and honey, I've a mother in my veins
who's a prompter to every line
I stump up, every image I connect
to making my life poetry
through the exchange rate, I can write you out
of my existence like a taser gun
firing a thought-shape, a thunder-blue cloud
into your face, mister I ain't got time,
but need your cash, I want a pink jumper,
some books, some music, Fortnum's tea,
and it's easier to sell my body
and still have time for poetry, than work
like you for an investment company',
the sky over his head like a cupcake
shot with shocking pink anatomy
of slo-mo smoothie cumulus blown right
towards Green Park, a black helicopter
doing surveillance like the military,
and all I want is money for my art
without concessions to the corporate draft
brainstorming youth into corrupt
Seroxat-fuelled dependency, the job

as a Shakespearean character
big as Canary Wharf inside the brain,
at least a blowjob liberates
me into uncompromised reality
my own cellular architecture
out of which I organize poetry
ejaculated by a mean punter
into a currency, he shares a trace
of semen in the poem's mix,
it's permanent inside my books, a dose
of degrading elevation
like a toxic smear, but I'm sure Marlowe
gagged over lines academics
don't treat as deep throat eloquence, just words
lifted like high rise into song
as sometimes 15th-century poetry
smelling of damp Sweet Williams
clumped back of a house, like I write today
lower than anything can come up right,
but snapdragons, the fleshy red ear lobes
totemic flower icons signalling
data to the bee's black nose cone,
while I do poetry like Sudoku,
thinking how earlier in Gerry's flat
I'd seen a slice of life like carrot cake
streaming in orange sunlight, got a flash
of altered physics in the dusty light
like mirror neurons firing up—
the place Kimberley St, Covent Garden
recording for the Ginger Light
in a bedroom with an aqua window
turned brilliant at 1 a.m.
by dazzle and Gerry's filigreed care
with me and sound, a piece of life
cut almost triangularly like toast,
slanting in with photons, his jar
of M&S strawberry jam a red
that pulls association with the toast
and stuck on it bits of my past, the stuff
glittered enough to recognize

as dissociated footage, dead facts
still there in the reversed future
as loss and damage, Gerry's pasta twirls
looking like DNA extracts
in a nutritional value packet,
his kitchen a place where the light collects
its information like a recipe
of atomized ingredients, his sauce
Tesco's tomato and basil, the red
of a nuclear flameout sun
gunning down over a radiated planet
onto the pigment of my hand.
Today the info in my poetry
its inspirational oxygen
addresses Posh's black push up bra cups
down from 34DD to 34B
reductionist taupe-coloured tit, a loss
in aesthetic, I like her blonde
and Manga lippy, she's the look I need
for upgraded lyric glucose,
size zero, prototypical android,
turning my imagery sexy,
like the poem morphs into her nipple's
indigo areola,
and follows curves sprayed in Versace jeans
as mapping of its geography
to saturation, like her lipstick line
bleeds into a red suffusion
hotter than art, her gamine petulance
the point of why I write today
on oppressive cloud-choked Marchmont Street
Saturday, peeled like an artichoke
to Posh's poppy-red defiant pout
as chutzpah for my poetry,
Posh in her vermilion-soled Christian Lacroix
spikes, like a poem on a stem,
turns fizzy in me rain checking metre
to feel the poem's torque, the give
like centimetres of a black g-string
escaped her jeans; the bite's like that

into the rhythm, I don't care
except to elevate Posh into top
quotient for the look in poetry,
my look, the one I ascribe to
as synonymous with an edgy line
from Kit Marlowe to Banksy's blocks
of hot pink attacking a city space
his poetry a lacerating slash
of optimistic takeover, a surge
of why don't you do right (BABY)—
a spray can one-liner laureate,
art terrorist to the corporates,
the city prowler turning on a van
or wall to urban jungle colouring
a DMDA saturated schlock
of black and red fantastic, or a green
like chemically synthesized crocodile
or blues that dye the sky denim
and ache with being all there is as blue
within that menu: Posh on scent—
Miller Harris *eau de parfum*—single note scent—
Philosophy, Creed and Floris,
'for nail colour, I recommend either
the colour of the season or deep red;'
a Nars beige on fingers and toes
makes both look longer with a clear topcoat
to curtail chipping: a poem's the same,
I fix the colour, photoshop the rest
and leave it to deteriorate
less seriously. I couldn't give a fuck
for poetry, www.jeremyreed.uk.com
won't give you answers, only that I read
Victoria Beckham's That Extra Half of an Inch
as a poetry anthology
to boost my serotonin: I do luck
with reported sightings, I tell you man
over Starbucks' ginger biscuits,
organic wheatflower, organic sunflower oil,
organic ground ginger 1.8%
that Michael Jackson's death from Demerol

and Oxylontin was a drop in's death
a post-biological alien's
window back to the purple star,
8st 11b of chemicalised projection
behind Grace Kelly blackouts, and the red,
the blood red of 1950s lipsticks,
mixed like a painter to red,
so demonstrably glam it was the Russian flag
rewritten Hollywood vermilion
in a lapsed inconsistent heart-shaped bow,
the light addressing him from out the hills
as just a shot away, a UFO flyover
warping his faux mansion's space-time
with parallel info, a Michael Kink
in which the light rayed-out purple
as a parabola he danced into
for no-one, but a reflective mirror
in which he impacted a shooting star
of weird excruciating loneliness,
the dancer always overtaking time
to end up terminally lonelier
with all those air miles in his blood
as liquid oxygen, his dance
like bubbles travelling light in champagne
meeting no resolve from the hips
throwing shapes like g-forces onto grooves
too hypnotic to connect to
without morphing into helium lift.
Of course Michael's more poetry
than poetry, I used to weigh 8 stone
at Piccadilly, waiting for the man,
the one who'd buy me into solvency,
the one in fifty rejected
for looks deficit, lack of tainted cash
and susceptible attitude,
I don't like corporate, fat, bankers, men
in creased misshapen suit jackets,
or rude, and only went with men who knew
that hurt is what makes poetry
into a terrorist free radical

a liberating embassy
of image in connect, the geography
assembled in hanging out there
a scandal I made into poetry—
the booze bill of Jimmy, a rogue MP,
who took me out in excess bravura,
1 jeroboam of Moët & Chandon Rosé
£8,000, 1 magnum of Dom Perignon
and shopping at Harrods 50 magnums
of Moët Rosé, £27,500,
Jimmy's optimal hedonistic groove
like a heist on department stores
a sexy plastic access to cute brands,
he bought me jewel-coloured cashmere jumpers
from the Burlington Arcade,
silvers like Brighton on a foggy day
blues pulled out of airport skies,
a pink like cerise carnations, a white
like 1950s retro queer,
a black like fashionista attitude,
intolerable cool and mean,
a Dilly railings black, and Jimmy drank
Sputnik vodka with pink champagne
on disinformed expenses, and his clothes
were saturated in Creed Vetiver,
I never knew him less than expensive
the way some get generic luck
to squirt money in impulsive surges
of orgasmic dopamine
into shopping addiction, Jimmy's drug,
his pleasure purchase oxygen,
so pink pounded it coloured strawberry
in a Harrods assistant hand
clammed to a black American express
Jimmy used as serious support
to qualify money as personality,
his only claim to occupying space
in afternoons, a privileged West End man
doing sophisticated bling
at Fortnum's Harvey Nicks, Harrods Food Hall,

stockpiling things against a sky
indifferently choked up with Knightsbridge clouds
accumulated for a day
nobody remembers in 1985,
a white sky turned abstract,
and I remember the assistant's scarlet bra,
two vermilion satin ribbons
measuring out 300 gms Tarry Souchang
in Harrods Food Hall, coffee skin
weightlessly tracked by strawberry straps,
the detail sticking, and the tea
smelling like smoked figs and expensive leather,
and something different in that day,
a red bra, smoky tea, a detached cloud
shaped like the hypothalamus
doing cloud sculpture, 1985
deleted like the contents of a fridge
updated weekly, I prefer Waitrose
as vegan friendly, and do fridge
to find the years labelled like wine bottles,
1981, Park Crescent,
my white façaded Nash apt block,
the olive green Venetian blinds
open like jungle slatterns on the day,
Marie making me up like a pop star
to work the West End writing poetry
into the Dilly interface,
and I getting autopsied in reviews
spat out with malicious venom,
so personal, I've stayed out of poetry
a lifetime, slapped so vehemently hard,
I've never felt I belonged anywhere
but under the stairs with outlaws
with no purchase on literature
no hope of ever scoping out
easier than I do, just the blank wall
of anonymity and rain
and sneering acrimonious contemporaries
fucking each other over with prizes
and editorial juju,

I mean I only carry poetry,
not African disease, just the best imagery
you'll get ever, an image magician
as good as psilocybin
or MOMA taken in the rain
to give the buildings skin,
I'm Londonimage, purplesugar.com
writing the streets into my veins
for text, I've got Harrods and Harvey Nicks
sited in my hippocampus,
the Ritz in my forehead, and Selfridges
sunk in my hypothalamus,
the city's monoliths metabolized
as urban lyric chemistry—
I own the lot in shares working the line
as an outlaw, a subverter
of corporate owned geography, the blood
soaked into London sites, a red
like pitting cherries, and today I read
on Soho steps, outside Blake's house,
on Marshall Street, tucked behind Newburgh Street,
a soundboarded opposite wall
attracting rogue foot traffic, audience
lazing sunnily on the steps
with bottles of Becks, I could feel the time
arrive like a Boeing checked in
from somewhere on the airwaves 3 a.m.,
I get around you know, these streets
are always in me, and I read
my poems everywhere it suits
to disrupt convention, a ruby shower
of sequins detonating from a hand
as I read 'Thieves Like Us (Baby Love)'
just down from where a friend raids Liberty
as compulsive Kleptomania,
an adrenalised grab at random things
finding neural correlatives in paste,
Diptych scents, scarves, a purple knitted tie,
soaps, any lux accessory
that binds to dopamine to get him high

as bits of CO^2 polluted green
transparent zones of Soho sky, I like
system subversions, Billy's knack
of downloading trouble before the eyes.
I read the poem like he's won
to lose, and yet it's loss fills his pockets,
and sadness overtakes my lines,
my voice—in knowing he's in rehab now
broken and on a learning graph
useless as picking up a paper plane
to relaunch it to America
his rhinestone glamour crunched by discipline,
otiose institutional
insensitivity to theft as clean
recreation, and 'Nifty Jim'
and all my fucked up Blakean pantheon
that get another life in me
for sexing my youth with aberrant ways,
and thanks, it gave me poetry
like finding a scratched diamond in the dark
as a reclaimed identity,
and I grew troubled, defiant, at war
with institutions, like I am
today, a Soho aficionado with style
and ambiguous sexuality—
as full of poetry as a ripe orange
loaded with vitaminised imagery,
and look, I give you everything
as nothing, something's good, a metaphor
dissolved like sugar in coffee,
a little sign, graffiti does it better
—arrive at Centre Point Food Stores—
the graffito's buried his font in paint
buddleia purple slashed on blue
a fuchsia cerise submerged in yellow,
it's how most people think of poetry
as buried slash, if there's meaning the feel
is all of it, (I eat a lemon cake)
between poems, polenta and drink wine
out of the bottle neck, I know

the way it goes, and how words get re-set
inside a poem, communication's
so simple, listen to the Pretty Things
and how Phil lifts it from the street—
'everything I'm given/something's taken back',
his ambivalent 'LSD'
as drug or money, and their right on sound
so hot it's punk in 1964,
and those songs come up in spaces between
my reading, 'Don't Bring Me Down',
'Honey I Need', 'Can't Stand the Pain',
like an implanted MP3,
I can't ever live without Phil's disdain,
his lippy R&B intransigent sneer
travelling up decades into my cells
as phrasing, a disruptive swipe
at suits and institutional PR
and fat cat scams, a London band
so hard and fast, they're designed-in
as sonic features—'tell me some more'
and still they'll die playing, resilient,
brilliant as a scarlet throw
on a black bed. The Pretties lost and won
and keep on winning with each play,
as deadly serious in their world, as me
to minimally cult poetry—
you win a reader once in twenty years
and lose him in an hour, a day,
but still the idea of poetry
persists like fog above the hills
as a blue smoky rumour, hangs in there
like a pop hook, a used-up theme
that resonates when the delivery's
ten years back, and ten years forward,
it equalizes somewhere on the way
as misfit poetry. Today
my 10 ten thunder-sky purple lissianas
given me from Old Street's McQueens
do tantra in my flat, soupy August,
polluted cloud smudging the sun

to a burnt orange disc, and I do herbs,
the Chinese ones fine-tuning orgasm
to optimal sensation, combining
split quantities of powder tweaked
to itchy acute sensitivity,
a supernova explosion,
the herbalist getting the pop in Chinatown
of how you work the ingredients
to a responsive chemistry
I call Li Po Orgasmic Activate
for fucking or a solo hand.
It all comes back again to poetry
as the active ingredient
canned over town, poetry's my graffiti bomb
tagged on the navel, it comes out of me
like a snake-twist of Kundalini
burning through the chakras or a bike
maxed on the motorway. Mostly I write
like it' s my last day every day,
gunning the expectation imaginatively
because it's all so little time,
like noticing the purple buddleia
and its hot sticky scent like fig
and a hot stationary Jaguar,
and knowing the ultimate rush
of living in the mauve tusk's transient
pop single duration, 3 weeks
of burning violet crumbled into orange.
The Ginger Light, we're on again,
myself and Itchy Ear, voice and laptop,
dominating the ICA—
poetry and electro-cabaret
pulling the audience into my voice
like coercive fellatio,
the poetry working an edge
that cherry-bites reality
for every colour in the mix
of London lowlife and its diamond edge
of compassion amongst the weird
as our modality—we do our set

the black stage drenched in green sequins
www.jeremyreed.co.uk
to refresh moments that were hot
as anything you get in poetry,
two camp desperados throwing
energies under a blue light.
Today I sit out under stonewashed skies
at Starbucks on Great Marlborough Street
my eye attracting detail and my look
attention: a black ruffled string
arched like an eyebrow above skinny jeans
drawing me into singular focus
and the single grey hair in the dense black
texturing of this Korean girl's
so sexy, a filigree thread
odd as a poem in its sit
in white space, but so provocative
you'd love her for that grey outtake
and never tell her it's like diamond
in its alluring sensual pull
into erotics; the detail's dissolved
by noting M&S roses,
the deep red of crushed raspberries
somebody's brought to alter mood,
I mean roses do quick sex with the eye
they're so optimal sensual,
they're more for eating than looking, I mean
it's like kissing an Asian blonde,
the ultimate erotic teaser to
quintessential orgasm: I phone
Gem, and she's fencing with gingers
and bruised pink stargazers at Seven Dials
arranging flowers at Wild Bunch, the way
colour rays out in frequencies
and throws a concentrated shape
of purples, pinks and blues.
Gem's a London jewel with her Mac makeup
glam artistry, a turquoise line
graduating to pencilled black,
and look a red hydrangea

the colour of strawberry summer pudding
gets shafted into flaky blues
and uh, a white with a rust beauty spot
wins background, there on Earlham Street,
with me still believing that poetry's
more important than oxygen
in sustaining its 1% readers.
You'd think there's something better I could pack
into my blood than imagery
that's simply flagrant theft without arrest
a right in your face robbery,
I mean that third beauty spot, left side cheek,
staggered like chocolate traffic lights
I've got in my focus and select
the one that's avocado shaped
and recreate it without permissions,
you'll never know you're my detail
or ever read a brand poem with Mac
and Clarins rival metaphors, and reds
doing instant Ferrari whine
on lips I've pulled from magazines
to get a shine. Sometimes it all goes wrong
and a skewed poem dumps its loss
like titanium. It's only a Marc Almond song
refocuses my damaged world
with its lived-in indigo saturation,
its torchy unilateral affair
with inconsolably disruptive loss,
his voice pitting pain like a black cherry,
you never get the love you need
so write or sing about the one you want
because the lack's creative luck,
I'll lose you aha, but I need to try
and knowing there's no going back
turn a gold hand to poetry,
a spot gold index 1,000 per troy ounce
below pivotal psychological level,
you try it offshore honey, a blue sea
encouraging safe assets, Comex gold,
Mizuho Securities, South Korea's Kospi,

the global markets walked on like a beach
Australia's S&P/ASX 200,
a spike in price to US900 an ounce,
it doesn't affect poetry
except gold's there as mineral in my veins,
a pink fog dusting a grey sea
in Jersey, two walk by the Shell-sloganed docks
with Android phones, the energy
from a waste incinerator polluting light,
red cranes like bonsai in a berth
that's bottle green, a hedge trust fraudster
and a septum-holed mafia
coke and gold addicted barrister
do futures and a drug dealer
on their phones, use Wikitude and Layar
directional sensors, look through their apps
as a fingertip alien. I go
back to my mist-finned island so little,
it's virtual as the coronae
fracturing Venus, or three days away
the moon's concrete coloured mashed regolith
but it's a Boeing surge over
a lapis lazuli channel, one drink
and twenty-five minutes later,
a granite pretzel swims in the window
no bigger than an arroyo,
an offshore, off-brand legitimised cell
a money ecosphere, you have
anonymous accounts for oligarchs,
and a Chinese puzzle of lanes
with sunken farms and manors sealed like forts
into a video-alert
motion-sensored plutocracy,
but there's black butter, and a potato
shaped like the moon, and sensually
rose-scented as a flushed Sancerre,
a taste that's tangy like seaweed,
the skin dusted with minerals
and licked by iodine salinity,
rare as gold nuggets, blotchy ovoids

flipped like black gold out of the April soil
the sky chilly as a freezer
the rain accelerating in a shower
striped like a rainbow, shimmery
from the Gulf of St Malo, rain's in it,
sparkling Brittany rain in potato,
you taste the sky in everything
grows in an island, and by June
the freckled ovals are replaced by royals,
a chunkier more solid taste
of deep earth roots, a retro-spuddy taste
of something just that rootier
and yellower and fully earthed
like a vegetable meteor
dug out of St John's, it's like middle earth
as a manorial parish
a rusty key to its sealed gates buried
under an oak's twisted torso.
I sat there in fluffy blue topaz fog
with Asa Benveniste, spaghetti thin,
black-shirted, moonstone ring, the kabala
mixed in his language, a word-soup
in which the alphabet swam like noodles
that steamed up into poetry,
Asa the maestro printer and poet
the eye that sanctioned Trigram Press,
there to fire gold in my teen poetry,
I was the poet he compared
to Rimbaud with my shook up imagery
and Jagger body, and his voice
pitched through blue toasted Camel smoke
was baritone cool like Leonard Cohen's
a generational 50s chilled out tone,
understated and lyrical,
a voice that unzipped women, it was silk
climbing like a morning glory
to poetry. We sat and crows convened
with their dodgy runic vocabulary
and threw black shapes, leather parabolas
through puffs of fog, the no-colour sky

like tonic drizzled into gin, the farm
a granite block in the valley,
an unworked, off-limits intelligence
secured by a tax-fraudster drugs cartel.
Asa chainsmoked his softpack Lucky Strike
his language doing smoke signals,
nicotine semiotics, he wanted
a book from me, my formative
clotted implosions, hallucinated,
done for sensation imagery,
and I, already neural in my search
to kick poetry into near sci-fi
wrote like dirty-bombing the dictionary
into my face, tattooed with words
stuck to me epidermally
like subjective iron crosses
that glittered with the tacky paste I wore
badged on my jacket in splashes
of ruby, green and nectarine.
Asa spoke of Trigram as poetry
subverting mainstream arteriosclerosis,
his travelled via Black Mountain
to New York fusion, pop and poetry,
Frank O'Hara and Bob Dylan jet-stream
free-associated, psychoactive
cocktail-shaken upended imagery,
magic, hoodoo and snake venom
appointed to the line, a stoned cowboy
appearing out the sun. We spoke of death
as Burroughs, the figure of death
as neural hologram, virtual junky,
an opiated infra-red
heroin-cuffed emissary, shoot death
into your veins like kerosene
into a plane, Bill put the skin on death
and a 3-piece Savile Row suit,
a Burlington Arcade cashmere jumper
in foggy blue or tin drum grey,
Asa collected detail like I do
and lived on a yoghurt a day,

Turkish coffee, Jack Daniels, J&B,
compact non-filter cigarettes
like Camel, Players, Lucky Strike, Pall Mall;
the field slowly emptied of mist
like a chilled bottle thawing, and more crows
appeared in primal diagrams
round a trio of colour-saturated oaks,
aggressive in their gutturals
as an Elizabethan madrigal.
Asa was the King's Cross cult publisher,
Tom Raworth *The Big Green Day*
Barry Cole *Vanessa in the City*
(long poem with a view)
Anselm Hollo *The Coherences*
(long and short poems by the master)
David Meltzer *Yesod*
(tracings of the invisible documents)
Asa Benveniste *The Atoz Formula*
(poems full of language and other ways)
Jim Dine *Welcome Home Lovebirds*
(Dine's first poems with drawings)
Jack Hirschman *Black Alephs*
(collected poems/ the real kabala)
Piero Heliczer *The Soap Opera*
(underworld book hard to forget)
B.S. Johnson *Poems Two*
(poetry that tastes of fig)
Nathaniel Tarn *October*
(the russet anthropologist)
Oswell Blakeston *How To Make Your Own Confetti*
(first Trigram book gritty and rare)
John Esam, Anselm Hollo, Tom Raworth *Haiku*
(three books multiple meaning)
Gavin Ewart *Gavin Ewart's Show*
(specially bound in flesh):
Asa's selling points in brackets; we sat
islanded by telepathy,
our juju register immediate,
our transfer like the speed of light,
my little completed by his sentences,

the sea up somewhere in the sky
as a jade puddle He gave me his book
The Atoz Formula, his language soaked
in printer's ink and occult imagery
like spooning gold dust from a jar
into imaginative chemistry.
Asa breathed language palpably
as smoke directed through his nostrils
under an antlered oak's twisted torso
the tree practicing green yoga
rooted into one position
of photosynthesis. Asa spoke likes,
mostly Tom Raworth for his speed
and rushed synaptic imagery
like jewels shot through the veins
into adrenal energy
as coloured minerals. I count them up
my Asa letters, all black ink
as black as liquorice, I've 53
from London and Fakenham,
Leverton Street and Blue Tile House, letters
that came with books: our Jersey day
a white horse sipping at its blue shadow,
plane traffic rumbling in the sky,
the leather strap of Asa's black daybag
looped like a snake, our chosen site
this oak's green umbrella pitched at a sky
vibrating constantly with turbo
throttling back, deaccelerated roar
of skyways, and his lighter flame
snapped periodically into a surge
of orange-blue Benzedrine.
I read *The Atoz Formula* for weeks
instructed by its coded imagery
into a new poetic DNA,
a larynx shaping words by cellular
respiration, lowercase stems
and columnar blocks, the shapes
helically diagrammatic like sex,
showing me linguistic fuck,

the poem written like fellatio
orgasmic in its metric scale;
and Asa's *Poems from the Mouth*,
more like an oriental 69
in tricky metaphysics, deep throat stuff
worked in phoneme orbit, poetry
as work, a molecular thing
that got into me intravenously
from Asa's blue ophidian brushstrokes,
the poem erect like a cock or snake
and chartable by chakras
if you search their porous meridians.
Asa in London, Kentish Town,
a silver crew-neck, a Camel sighting
from obsidian ash tray,
his first scotch poured at 10.30am,
a twinkly amber Jack Daniels,
he'd got a manuscript from J.H. Prynne
a cool postmodern refrigerated
anti-narrative written at Ed Dorn's
no subject matter, just the thing
alien as an urinanalysis
with a sexy tone, a Prynne
semiotic abstraction, blue and red
if you see colours in a block
of chewing gum coloured poetry,
and Asa did in *News of Warring Clans*,
took it for tangential odd
and its impenetrable matte,
a Cambridge/US fusion, specific
as a Toshiba accountant.

www.ingramcontent.com/pod-product-compliance
Lightning Source LLC
Chambersburg PA
CBHW021327190426
43193CB00039B/313